Intimate Moments for Couples

RICHARD EXLEY

VALLEW
PRESS

Intimate Moments for Couples
ISBN 0-97851-376-2

P.O. Box 54744
Tulsa, Oklahoma 74155

Published by Vallew Press
P.O. Box 35327
Tulsa, Oklahoma 74153-0327

DEDICATION

To Brenda Starr,

my best friend, my lover, my wife.

In good times and bad

you have been the light of my life.

You are my favorite person in all the world,

and the co-author of my most important work—life.

CONTENTS

INTIMATE
MOMENTS
FOR COUPLES

ONE
Beginnings

SECTION 1
BEGINNINGS

In reality, marriage is both a gift and a discipline. God gives us each other and the tools for cultivating our blessed oneness, but it is up to us to work the soil of our relationship all the days of our life.

"There will be the inevitable conflicts, little hurts and not so little hurts, bitter quarrels and haunting fears. Pressures too, which pull at us, causing us to drift apart. Silences beneath our words, and loneliness which only those who have known the blessed oneness can imagine. Holy moments too when forgiveness gives birth to intimacy, when the silences and the separation are put behind us, and once again we know who we are and where we belong.

"In truth, marriage is a lot like life—full of contradictions and conflicts, but for all of that still so blessed, oh so blessed. It has its moments—anniversaries and other special days, as well as unscheduled surprises and unexpected kindnesses, little gestures of love which set the heart to singing—but, for the most part, it's more pedestrian. And it's those mundane details which mold the character of our relationship. Little things, which at first glance seem hardly worth mentioning. Yet as the years go by, they become daily rituals.

"I mean, who even speaks of the simple pleasure of coming home to familiar sounds—the hum of the vacuum cleaner, bath water running, conversation from the other room—yet these are the sounds of marriage. And the smells—skin cream and shampoo, clothes fresh from the dryer, furniture polish and coffee brewing. Ordinary things easily taken for granted, hardly noticed, until they are gone."[1]

—Richard Exley

REAL MEN DON'T EAT MALT-O-MEAL

Brenda sat on the edge of the bed coaxing me into wakefulness, and as sleep fled it all came rushing back—the wedding, our first night together at the historic Warwick Hotel in Houston, and breakfast in our room. There had been linen napkins, real china and silver, and a single red rose in a crystal vase. That was the extent of our honeymoon; it was all we could afford, just one extravagant night in the Warwick, but it was worth every penny it cost. Now it was over, and we were in our own small apartment beginning our first day of real marriage.

"You look wonderful," I said, rubbing sleep from my eyes. And she did. Her dark brown hair was brushed, and she had put on makeup. I experienced a moment of gratefulness as I thought of spending the rest of my life with this beautiful woman.

Grabbing my hand she said playfully, "Get up, lazybones. I've made you breakfast, but I'm not going to serve you in bed."

I'm not sure what I expected, bacon and eggs maybe, with a cup of steaming black coffee. After all, that's what Mom made for my dad. What I didn't expect was a candle-lit breakfast served on china, but that's what I got.

Trying to appear nonchalant, I took my seat and surveyed the table. "What's this?" I asked, pointing at a cereal bowl containing a foreign-looking substance.

There must have been something in the tone of my voice because Brenda gave me a hurt look before she replied. "That's Malt-o-Meal," she said. "It's my dad's favorite."

"Malt-o-Meal," I said, not even trying to hide my disgust. "Real men don't eat Malt-o-Meal."

Brenda was more than a little peeved by this time, but she did her best to remain calm. "Well, at least have some toast," she said, offering me a slice.

Trying to be civil myself, I smiled thinly and took a slice, only to be blindsided again. "What kind of toast is this?" I demanded. "It's only toasted on one side, for heaven's sake!"

"It's oven toast," she said through gritted teeth, "and if you don't like it, you don't have to eat it."

Without another word I left the table and headed for the shower. Slamming the bathroom door, I leaned against the wall muttering to myself. "Malt-o-Meal and one-sided toast," I fumed, "what kind of breakfast is that?"

What we have here is a classic example of newlywed bliss falling prey to immaturity and the reality of marriage. Without realizing it, I expected Brenda to be like my mother. At least I expected her to cook breakfast the way my mother did. For her part, Brenda expected me to be like her father, at least in the things I liked to eat.

Like many newlyweds, we discovered that we had distinctly different models for marriage. Although both of us were reared in Christian families with the same basic values, there were still many individual differences; differences that put no little strain on our young marriage. The challenge for us, as it is for most newlyweds, was to give up our parental models for marriage and together develop one that was uniquely our own.

ACTION STEPS

- Think about your parental model for marriage. Identify five or six specific characteristics. What are its strengths and weaknesses? Are there any characteristics that you would like to incorporate into your own marriage? If so, what are they?

- Now consider your own marriage. Have you developed a model that is uniquely suited to the two of you or are you still clinging to your parental model? What changes would you like to make?
- In prayer ask God to make you the kind of husband/wife that your spouse needs. Give God permission to change you.

THOUGHT FOR THE DAY

"The bride and groom have successfully left home. They're on their own. But the home has not left them.

"The old patterns from home color nearly everything in the new marriage. Do you open gifts on Christmas Eve or Christmas morning? Do you make your bed immediately upon rising or when you go through the house tidying up? The way you did it when you were growing up is right, of course. Any other way, though not exactly wrong, isn't right either."[2]

—Dr. Frank and Mary Alice Minirth

—Dr. Brian and Dr. Deborah Newman

—Dr. Robert and Susan Hemfelt

SCRIPTURE FOR THE DAY

"For this reason a man will leave his father and mother and be united to his wife, and they will become one flesh."

—Genesis 2:24

PRAYER

Lord, I can't believe how selfish and immature I can be at times. Forgive me for sinning against my spouse and against my marriage. Change me. Make me the kind of husband/wife that I should be. In the name of Jesus I pray. Amen.

TRANSCENDING OUR DIFFERENCES

How can two people grow up in the same town, attend the same church, graduate from the same high school, go together for five years and still not know each other when they marry? I can't answer that, but I can tell you that Brenda and I are living proof that it is possible. To further complicate this mystery, Brenda went on vacation with my parents and me in Colorado, and I spent Christmas with Brenda and her parents at her grandparent's farm on more than one occasion. I mean, we should have known each other, but we didn't.

Consequently, the first few months of our marriage were a real adventure. It seemed that hardly a week went by without one of us discovering some new area of incompatibility. For instance, Brenda's family ate only one family meal a day, and the rest of the time it was everyone for himself At our house, we ate three meals a day, and by the clock. Imagine my dismay when Brenda informed me that she would be preparing only one meal each day. To make matters worse, there wouldn't be a scheduled mealtime either. She was the cook, and she would cook when it best suited her schedule.

Then there was the coffee. I grew up in a home where coffee is serious business. The first thing Mother did when she got up in the morning was go to the kitchen and get the percolator going. Then she started breakfast; by the time my father entered the kitchen, after finishing his shower and dressing for work, there was a steaming cup of that dark brew waiting for him. Of course, I expected Brenda to follow in Mom's footsteps.

Wrong! Brenda's parents didn't drink coffee. Consequently, she never developed a taste for it. As far as she was concerned, coffee was not part of the marriage vows. To her way of thinking, he who drinks the coffee should also make it. And clean up the mess, I might add.

There's more, lots more, like breakfast on Sunday. Growing up, Brenda seldom ate breakfast, and never on Sunday. For me, Sunday breakfast was a family tradition. We usually had my brother Don's favorite, which was french toast and sausage, or Dad's—biscuits and gravy.

I tried to explain this to Brenda, but it was no use. Patiently she explained that there was absolutely no way she could cook breakfast and still be ready for church on time. At this point I made a near-fatal mistake. I pointed out to her that my mother had herself and four children to get ready for church, yet she still managed to fix a wonderful breakfast each Sunday. Giving me a look that could kill, Brenda said sweetly, "Well, I'm not your mother."

I've since learned that my dad was the one who fixed breakfast on Sundays. I don't know how I could have forgotten that salient fact, but I did. It just goes to show how selective our memories can be. Needless to say, that was the end of the discussion. I don't cook. Ever! And certainly not on a Sunday morning.

The issues I'm talking about here aren't really big things. They do, however, illustrate the kind of adjustments almost all couples face in the early days of their marriage. How you handle these housekeeping items will go a long way toward determining the emotional climate of your relationship.

There are three basic ways to resolve any conflict: 1) compromise, 2) agree to disagree, 3) give in. Finding the right solution to your particular conflict is one of the keys to developing a meaningful marriage.

Of course, different situations demand different solutions. In the case of daily meals, Brenda and I compromised. We now have two meals a day. When we eat them is flexible, depending on our schedules.

We never eat breakfast on Sundays. On this point I gave in; not grudgingly, but with good humor. Being a pastor, I decided that it was more important to have an attractive wife at my side on Sunday morning than to have a full stomach. Besides, my family has a history of heart disease, and I have to watch my cholesterol.

About the coffee, we agreed to disagree. I still think Brenda should make it, and she still thinks it's my responsibility. Generally, I brew my own coffee, but from time to time Brenda surprises me with a steaming cup of espresso, and when she does I feel especially loved.

On issues like these, there really isn't a right way or a wrong way. Rather, each couple must work out a system that is best for them. The sooner they do so, the sooner they can move on to more important things.

ACTION STEPS

- Make a list of the little things you argued about in the early days of your marriage. Looking back, doesn't it seem silly to have spent so much time and energy on such trivial matters?
- Now make a list of the unresolved issues in your marriage. How many of them are worth fighting about? Will they really matter five years from now, or ten?
- With God's help, determine right now to stop wasting valuable time and energy on unimportant matters.

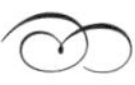

THOUGHT FOR THE DAY

"Marriage immediately forces changes upon the partners, which, no matter how well prepared they thought they were, surprise them and require a new and specialized labor from both of them. This is the fact: The woman does not know who her husband is until he is her husband, nor the man his wife until she exists as wife. Before the marriage these people were fiancés, not spouses; fiancés and spouses are different creatures, and the second creature doesn't appear until the first has passed away. Did the courtship last many, many years? It doesn't matter. Were they friends long before they initiated courtship? It doesn't matter. They still can't know the spouse until he or she is a spouse; and there isn't a spouse until there is a marriage.

"So the recently married couple has a job to do, a good job, a hopeful and rewarding job, but labor nonetheless. And it will take a patient, gentle energy to accomplish this labor well."[1]

—Walter Wangerin, Jr.

SCRIPTURE FOR THE DAY

"If you have any encouragement from being united with Christ, if any comfort from his love, if any fellowship with the Spirit, if any tenderness and compassion, then make my joy complete by being like-minded, having the same love, being one in spirit and purpose. Do nothing out of selfish ambition or vain conceit, but in humility consider others better than yourselves. Each of you should look not only to your own interests, but also to the interests of others."

—PHILIPPIANS 2:1-4

PRAYER

Lord, I'm so competitive. Everything becomes a matter of winning and losing, even my relationships. I have this insatiable need to be right, to win every argument, no matter who gets hurt. Forgive me for abusing the gift of competitiveness, for using it to get my own way. Give me the wisdom and the grace to use it constructively, and only in situations that really matter In the name of Jesus I pray. Amen.

MARRIAGE MYTHS

"Marriage is in trouble today," according to Reformed pastor Frederick Herwaldt, Jr., "because society and the church have a faulty view of it, a myth of this human, delightful, yet flawed, institution. Though a few lone voices speak against the institution, most laud a romantic image of marriage as life's ultimate source of true joy."[1]

Think about it for a minute and I believe you will agree with him. We enter marriage with such bright expectations and high hopes. Parents shed bittersweet tears of painful happiness. Friends laugh, hug our necks and congratulate us. It's a special moment, holy and happy. We have vowed our faithfulness "till death do us part." We belong to each other as we have never belonged to anyone before. She is our only wife. He is our only husband. In all the other relationships of our life, we are one among many. Not now, not here! For the first time ever, he or she is the only one to us, and we are the only one to him or her.

Yet, how quickly the magic of the wedding is replaced by the reality of living together day after day. Our starry-eyed romanticism is confronted with a one-bedroom apartment, an unbelievably tight budget and the irritating habits of a spouse who can only be described as insensitive. What makes all of this so difficult is that it is very different from what we were led to expect.

The truth is, as Herwaldt points out, most of the things we initially believe about marriage are myths. Myths, which produce unrealistic expectations, thus setting us up for disappointment. One of the most prevalent of these is what I call the "Marriage Made in Heaven" myth. It's the one that says if you marry the person God has chosen for your mate, you will live "happily ever after."

Nothing dispels this myth faster than the biblical story of Isaac and Rebekah. Abraham sent his most trusted servant back home to select a wife for his son Isaac from among his own people. When the servant arrived at the town of Nahor, it was near evening, about the time when the women went out to draw water.

"Then he prayed, 'O Lord, God of my master Abraham, give me success today, and show kindness to my master Abraham.... May it be that when I say to a girl, "Please let down your jar that I may have a drink," and she says, "Drink, and I'll water your camels too"—let her be the one you have chosen for your servant Isaac.'...

"Before he had finished praying, Rebekah came out with her jar on her shoulder...

"The servant hurried to meet her and said, 'Please give me a little water from your jar.'

"'Drink, my lord,' she said.... 'I'll draw water for your camels too, until they have finished drinking.'"[2]

You couldn't ask for clearer direction, or a stronger confirmation, than that. As Rebekah's parents said, "...This is from the Lord...."[3]

Yet, the marriage of Isaac and Rebekah was far from ideal. They were incompatible. Isaac favored their older son Esau while Rebekah favored the younger son Jacob, and this was a source of constant tension between them. Their marriage reached a low point when Rebekah helped Jacob trick his blind and aging father in order to steal Esau's inheritance. There's more, but I'm sure you get the point.

Couples who embrace this myth run at least two risks. First, they are tempted to take their marriage for granted. They mistakenly believe that since it was made in heaven it will be great without any effort on their part. This, of course, results in a less than perfect marriage, which leads to the second temptation. Once the marriage starts to fall apart it is easy to conclude that the marriage was a mistake.

While marrying God's chosen mate does not guarantee you a good marriage, neither does marrying the wrong person destine you to failure. Once you marry, all thoughts about the rightness or wrongness of your choice should be put out of your mind. If you will both commit yourselves to God and to the marriage, you can have a fulfilling relationship even if you did marry the "wrong person."

Good marriages don't just happen, not even when each partner marries the right person. They are the product of the combined efforts of two committed people and God—two people who have chosen to make their marriage a high priority, who have decided that their spouse's happiness is more important than their own and who have determined that nothing shall undermine their relationship.

ACTION STEPS

Make a list identifying some of the expectations you brought into marriage. Be specific.

- Now examine them. Are they realistic? Have you given up the unrealistic ones or are they still a source of disappointment for you?
- In prayer ask God to help you formulate some realistic goals for your marriage. Discuss these with your spouse and get his/her comments.

THOUGHT FOR THE DAY

"Marriage may be 'made in heaven' in the original. But the whole deal is more like one of those kits which comes knocked down for putting together. It will take some gluing here, sanding rough spots there, hammering a bit now, filing down the scratches on this side, planing a bit on that side, carving a piece, bending this section slightly, varnishing, backing off for a frequent look, dusting, waxing, polishing, until at last what you have is a thing of beauty and a joy forever."[4]

—Charlie W. Shedd

SCRIPTURE FOR THE DAY

"Houses and wealth are inherited from parents, but a prudent wife is from the Lord."

—Proverbs 19:14

PRAYER

Lord, I have to confess that I often put unrealistic expectations on my spouse. I expect him/her to make me happy. I expect him/her to understand my needs when I can't even put them into words myself. I expect him/her always to respond to my desires no matter what is going on in his/her life. I expect too much! Help me to make up for all the times I've made him/her feel inadequate by expecting him/her to do what only You can do. In Jesus' name I pray. Amen.

THE MYTH OF ROMANTIC LOVE

As a young man growing up, I was told, "Don't marry the one you can live with. Marry the one you can't live without." Which was just another way of saying that the most important factor in a successful marriage is the feeling of being in love. Some people call that falling in love. By whatever term, it seems to refer more to a romantic, starry-eyed infatuation than the Bible's description of real love.

Infatuation is often mistaken for love because of its intense emotions, its strong sexual attraction and its romantic excitement. In short, infatuation is a feeling, while true love is a commitment that goes beyond romantic feelings. True love will have its romantic moments, and it should, but it takes more than moonlight and music to sustain a marriage.

When two people fall in love, they have a tendency to overlook faults in each other, to ignore danger signals and to dismiss the counsel of more objective persons. Once they marry, the things they ignored during courtship often come back to haunt them. If they are not careful, their differences can become a battlefield, and their love a casualty. Because they built their marriage on the faulty foundation of romantic love, they now risk divorce. Indeed, every year thousands of couples decide to end their marriage simply because the romance has gone out of their relationship. They married for the wrong reason, and now they are divorcing for an equally wrong reason.

Don't misunderstand me. I'm not suggesting that romantic love has no place in marriage, far from it. I'm simply saying that there are other factors to be considered when evaluating your marriage. Things like a shared faith, similar backgrounds, common goals, emotional resonance and God's will. These are the things that will sustain your marriage when the tough times come. Romantic love is simply the seasoning that adds flavor to all the rest.

ACTION STEPS

- Make a list of the things that characterize romantic love. List both emotions and actions. Give an example of romantic love in your marriage.
- Make a list of the things that characterize true, biblical love. List both emotions and actions. Give an example of this kind of love in your marriage.
- Discuss your findings with your spouse and talk about ways to integrate both kinds of love into your relationship. Be specific.

THOUGHT FOR THE DAY

"If you expect to live on the top of the mountain, year after year, you can forget it! Emotions swing from high to low in cyclical rhythm, and since romantic excitement is an emotion, it too will certainly oscillate."[1]

—Dr. James Dobson

SCRIPTURE FOR THE DAY

"Love is patient, love is kind. It does not envy, it does not boast, it is not proud. It is not rude, it is not self-seeking, it is not easily angered, it keeps no record of wrongs. Love does not delight in evil but rejoices with the truth. It always protects, always trusts, always hopes, always perseveres. Love never fails. . . ."

—I Corinthians 13:4-8

PRAYER

Lord, I tend to think more about being loved than I do about being loving. Forgive me, for that is not love at all, but selfishness. Teach me to love my spouse unconditionally, whether I feel loving or not, whether I am loved or not. Manifest Your love through me. In Jesus' name I pray. Amen.

PEOPLE CAN CHANGE, CAN'T THEY?

As a minister I have done a considerable amount of premarriage counseling. In the course of our sessions I inevitably ask each couple, "What do you like least about your fiancé? What habits does he/she have that get on your nerves?" As you might imagine, most engaged couples are uncomfortable with that line of questioning. They would rather talk about each other's good points. I call it the "ostrich complex." Pretend something is not there, and maybe it will go away.

I press them, and the tension mounts. He looks at her. She looks at him. They both look back at me. Silently, I wait with a half smile on my lips. Finally, she breaks the silence and divulges something, all the while being careful not to look at him. His face usually turns red, and he squirms uncomfortably in his chair.

"Do you think," I ask her, straight-faced, "that you can live with that for the next fifty years?"

Defensively, she responds, "People can change, can't they?"

Turning to him I ask, "Did you hear what she said?"

He looks puzzled, but replies, "She said people can change, can't they?"

"That's the words she used, but that's not what she said. She said that she has no intention of living with you the way you are. As soon as you two are married, she's going to remake you into the man she thinks you ought to be."

He looks at her incredulously, "Is that what you said?"

"Not really," she explains nervously, "I mean, it sounds so cruel when you put it that way." Gathering her courage, she plunges ahead, "But I don't expect you to keep your bad habits either. Surely you'll outgrow them."

A wise man would probably call the whole thing off right there, but then wisdom is not a virtue very often found in young, engaged men. Instead, he listens intently while I tell her that anything that bothers her during courtship will drive her absolutely mad after marriage. I explain that people do mature and that the maturing process brings about change, but that those changes seldom affect a person's annoying habits. She nods wisely, and he assumes that she has made peace with his idiosyncrasies. I know better. Even while we speak, she is plotting her post-wedding strategy.

In her book, *A Marriage Made in Heaven or Too Tired for an Affair,* Erma Bombeck confesses her own culpability. She admits that even as she and Bill were reciting their wedding vows she was thinking: "The man definitely needed work. But I had years ahead to mold him into the husband he was capable of being. First, I made a mental note to let his hair grow out. God, I hated his burr. It made him look like a shag rug that had just been vacuumed.

"And we'd have to do something about his eating habits. I came from a family that considered gravy a beverage. He ate vegetables, which I regarded as decorations for the mantel. Imagine spending the rest of your life with a man who had never had cold dumplings for breakfast!

"His best man and poker-playing buddy, Ed Phillips, passed him the ring. I smiled as Bill slipped it on my finger. Ed and the entire group of merry little men were soon to be part of the past. No more single life—playing poker until all hours of the morning. From here on in, it would just be the two of us, watching sunsets and gazing into one another's eyes.

"As our shoulders touched, I was challenged by the idea of setting up a schedule for him. All the years we had been dating, he had been late for everything. I was vowing to spend eternity with a man who had never heard the 'Star-Spangled Banner' or seen a kickoff at a game ... never watched a curtain go up or heard an overture. He looked so relaxed. He couldn't know that I would soon teach him the virtues of putting the cap on a ballpoint pen so that it wouldn't dry out and instruct him on how left-handed people are supposed to hang up the phone so they won't drive right-handed people crazy."[1]

Erma may be exaggerating things just a bit, but her point is well taken. Sooner or later most of us try to remake our spouse in our own image. When we read Erma's account we find it hilarious, but in real life it is an altogether different matter. As one wife said a year after the wedding, "During the engagement I was so afraid of losing him that, although I noticed a lot of things I did not like, I didn't say anything. I thought things would get better after the wedding. Now all we do is fight."

What is the source of their conflict, his behavior or her demands? That depends on the individual situation, of course, but more often than not it is her demands. When he doesn't meet them, she experiences anger. What she fails to realize is that the source of her anger and frustration is her demands, not her spouse's behavior.

This very behavior, the thing that is apparently driving her to despair, is not a new thing. It is not infidelity, or domestic violence or alcohol abuse. It is an annoying habit, like eating with his mouth open, nothing more. It was present during their courtship, and it did not make her angry then. Why? Because she did not demand that he change. It is the frustration of her demands then, not his behavior, that is the source of her anger.

The quickest way to resolve this dilemma and restore peace in the relationship is for her to release her demands. Accept him unconditionally, the way she did during their courtship. If change is really important to her, she should make it a matter of prayer. After all, only God can change another person. And when she prays, let her also ask God to change her, to make her the kind of wife He has called her to be.

ACTION STEPS

Make a list of the habits you would like your spouse to change. Now ask yourself the following questions:[2]

1) Are my expectations realistic?
2) Am I hurt in any way, shape or form if my spouse doesn't change this habit?
3) Is the changing of this habit essential to the attainment of any specific goal I have for my marriage?

4) Does my desire to see this habit changed affect my spouse's perception of me?

5) Does my need to see this habit changed achieve the kind of emotional responses I want for my spouse and me in our marriage?

If you answered no to three or more of these questions, your expectations are probably invalid. If any demand is valid, then approach your spouse in a new manner, such as: "I would appreciate it if you would..." or, "I would really prefer that you..."

THOUGHT FOR THE DAY

"Suddenly each spouse turns his eyes away from the partner, and looks inwardly and asks, 'What am I doing to my partner? What is wrong with me? What am I misunderstanding? What must I do to rescue this marriage?' If honestly asked the answers are not far behind: 'I really married my wife because of her difference. It is not my job to make her over, but rather to discover and value that difference .... How arrogant of me to think I could shape another human being! How humble it makes me to realize that I need to yield to another and thereby be changed! Our relationship will change both of us—in a process of being shaped into a form far more beautiful than either could imagine."[3]

—Abraham Schmitt

SCRIPTURE FOR THE DAY

"'For this reason a man will leave his father and mother and be united to his wife, and the two will become one flesh.' This is a profound mystery—but I am talking about Christ and the church. However, each one of you also must love his wife as he loves himself, and the wife must respect her husband."

—EPHESIANS 5:31-33

PRAYER

Lord, love is not demanding. Therefore, when I demand that my spouse change to please me, I am not acting in love regardless of how much I protest to the contrary. Forgive my arrogance, Lord. How presumptuous of me to think I always know what's right, what's best. Give me eyes to see the good and not the bad, and a heart filled with loving gratefulness. These are the gifts I am most in need of. In Your holy name l pray. Amen.

UNREALISTIC EXPECTATIONS

If you are like most newlywed couples, you entered marriage with high anticipation. You may not understand much about it, or the commitments you have made, but you do expect to be happy, and fulfilled and secure, and a whole host of other things as well.

Like the couples Aaron Rutledge describes in his book on premarital counseling you "…expect marriage to provide self-development and fulfillment; mutual expressions of affection; satisfaction of sexual urges; a sharing of child-rearing responsibilities; a mutual experience of status, belongingness and security; and shared interests in friends, recreation, worship, and creative work."[1]

In truth, you expect too much! A spouse can love you, listen to you and affirm you, but he or she cannot be responsible for your emotional well-being. Such unrealistic expectations set you up for disappointment, which often leads to despair, then resentment.

Is there an answer, a way of working through these disappointing times without giving up your dreams of a fulfilling marriage? Yes, but it will require you to reexamine your most fundamental beliefs about marriage.

There's nothing magical about matrimony. It will not suddenly transform you into something you are not. In fact, initially, marriage will probably reveal the worst about you and about your spouse, resulting in your unhappiness. Now you are faced with three choices: 1) you can blame your spouse and seek ways to punish him or her, 2) you can give up your dreams of a fulfilling marriage and just go through the motions, or 3) you can go to work on the marriage.

The first option is self-defeating. It accomplishes nothing. It only makes matters worse. The second option is a dead-end. It dooms your marriage to mediocrity. The third option is the only way, but it will be hard work indeed.

You must now come to terms with the fact that the key to success in marriage is not so much marrying the right person, but becoming the right person. You now accept that, at its heart, marriage is not about getting, but giving. Instead of seeking to have your needs met, you now focus on meeting your spouse's needs. Your labor of love is a gift that you give to God first, and then to your marriage.

Does this mean that your spouse will then respond in kind? Perhaps, but there are no guarantees. Besides, that is not why you are doing this. You are not looking for what you can get out of your marriage, or for what your spouse can do for you, but for what you can give to your marriage.

What we are really talking about is an act of faith, the courage to believe that if you really lose your life in loving obedience, you will ultimately find it.[2] The question you must answer is: "Do I dare to believe that God will take care of my personal needs if I will lose myself in loving service to Him and to my spouse?"

ACTION STEPS

- In prayer, make a conscious decision to serve your marriage and your spouse. Ask God to enable you to do this by the power of His Holy Spirit.
- Make a list of ways in which you can give of yourself to your marriage and your spouse without looking for anything in return. Be specific.

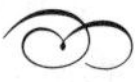

THOUGHT FOR THE DAY

"We live in days and times where words like 'sacrifice' and 'commitment' are four-letter words. I realize that, to many people, Kay's decision to love and honor her husband's wishes might seem unenlightened or even terribly wrong. After all, *she had her rights.* But as Kay was to find out, it was in laying down her rights that she finally broke through to her husband.

"In simple terms what Kay literally did was make love a decision. *Genuine love is honor put into action regardless of the cost.* It comes from a heart overflowing with love for God, freeing us to seek another person's best interests. Kay knew that only by loving God first and foremost could she ever hope to pull off loving John—especially after what he had done. Every 'instinct' she had told her to lash out. Yet in spite of her 'instincts,' her love would be based on a decision to honor her husband—not her emotions."[3]

—Gary Smalley

SCRIPTURE FOR THE DAY

"Wives, in the same way be submissive to your husbands so that, if any of them do not believe the word, they may be won over without words by the behavior of their wives, when they see the purity and reverence of your lives. Your beauty should not come from outward adornment, such as braided hair and the wearing of gold jewelry and fine clothes. Instead, it should be that of your inner self, the unfading beauty of a gentle and quiet spirit, which is of great worth in God's sight...

"Husbands, in the same way be considerate as you live with your wives, and treat them with respect as the weaker partner and as heirs with you of the gracious gift of life, so that nothing will hinder your prayers."

—I PETER 3:1-4,7

PRAYER

Lord, I'm afraid to surrender my rights in this marriage. I don't want to become a doormat. Yet, I have to admit that when I demand my rights we only end up fighting. Someone has to have the courage to change, and I guess it will have to be me. Give me the faith to trust You to meet my needs even as I "lay down my life" to meet my spouse's needs. In Jesus' name I pray. Amen.

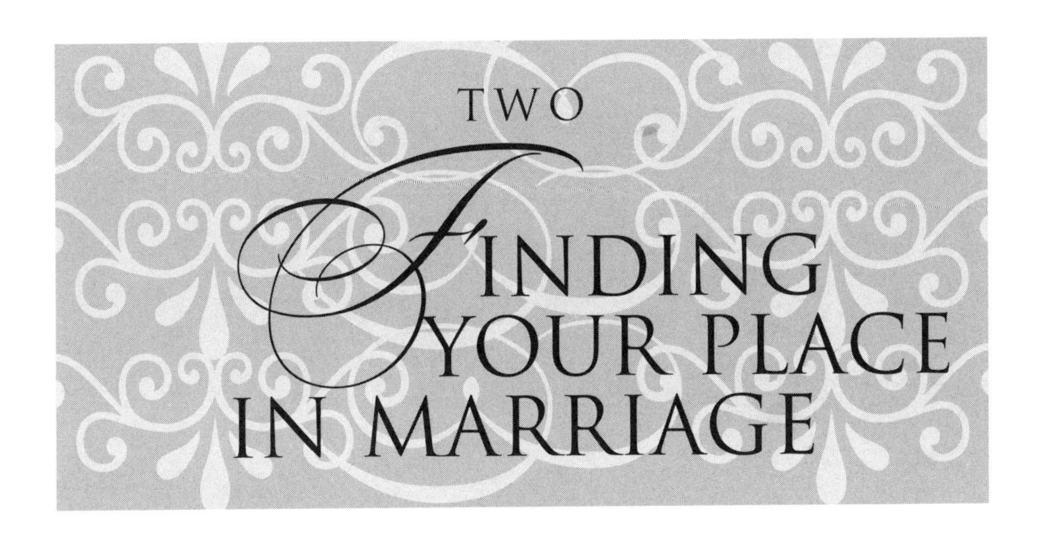

TWO
FINDING YOUR PLACE IN MARRIAGE

"Building a good marriage means that each person must take time to redefine roles, beliefs and behaviors and negotiate the differences with a partner. Use of space in the home, time, money, power, family traditions, rituals, friends, vocations are just a few of the issues which will be negotiated."[1]

—H. Norman Wright

DEFINING THE ROLES OF HUSBAND AND WIFE

For centuries, society provided a clear definition of roles for both men and women. Not anymore. The sexual revolution and the radical feminist movement have changed all of that. In an article for *Family Circle,* Ann Landers writes: "Even the most dimwitted clod should have noticed that by now American family life has undergone a metamorphosis that has made male and female roles almost interchangeable."[2] As a consequence, many couples experience both confusion and conflict as they try to find their place in marriage.

I'll be the first to admit that the tyrannical role many husbands and fathers have played for generations needed to be rewritten, but let me hasten to add that the redefining of roles for men and women in marriage need not, indeed must not, be equated with the abandonment of the scriptural roles for husbands and wives. Social customs must never replace the Word of God as our model for marriage.

While there are numerous passages of Scripture that give insight into the marriage relationship, none is quite as comprehensive as Ephesians 5:22-33. In this passage, wives are commanded to respect their husbands and to submit to them. Husbands are commanded to love their wives unconditionally and sacrificially, as Christ loved the church and gave himself up for her."[3]

Ephesians 5 is not an arbitrary ruling on roles for men and women in marriage; rather it is divine insight into the nature of men and women. Better than anyone else, God knows what makes us tick. He understands the unique needs each one of us has. On the basis of that insight, He inspired the apostle to define our roles in marriage in order to fulfill us as both individuals and as a couple.

God created men and women equal, but different. We are equal in value, but different in function and in our emotional makeup. If we approach Ephesians 5 with this understanding, it brings things into focus.

Husband, ask yourself, "Why does God want me to love my wife in the same way Christ loved the Church?" Because, by divine design, she can only be truly fulfilled when she is loved and cherished by you, her husband. Regardless of how much she is loved by family and friends, she will never feel truly complete unless she is secure in your love.

Wife, ask yourself, "Why does God command me to respect my husband and to submit to him?" For the same reason, of course. Your husband needs your respect in order to be fulfilled as a man. No matter how successful he becomes, no matter what position he attains, only your respect can truly make him feel like a man.

Now let's look at it in terms of roles. If a wife's greatest need is to be loved, then her husband's primary role in marriage is to love and cherish her. Similarly, if a husband's greatest need is to be respected by his wife, then her primary role in marriage is to honor and respect him. Nothing, it seems, could be simpler. Nevertheless, as you work to flesh out this principle in your marriage you will discover that it is easier said than done.

ACTION STEPS

For him:

- Ask your wife what you do that makes her feel loved. Listen closely to her response. Now make a conscious decision to do those things on a daily basis.

For her:

- Ask your husband what you do that makes him feel respected. Listen closely to his response. Now make a conscious decision to do those things on a daily basis

THOUGHT FOR THE DAY

"We were interested in seeing how often certain items occurred no matter how high or low they were on a person's list (of the ways they expected to receive love). Women mentioned hugs and kisses more than any other category; being listened to the next most often. The third most often listed category was verbal expression of love.

"The most frequently mentioned category for the men was the same as for the women: the expression of love through hugs and kisses. The second most often mentioned item for men was unconditional acceptance. (That, too, is consistent with what I have seen in similar surveys among married couples. The women have the hunger to be heard, to be taken seriously, and the men have the hunger to be accepted just as they are.)"[4]

—Rich Buhler

SCRIPTURE FOR THE DAY

'Wives, submit to your husbands as to the Lord. For the husband is the head of the wife as Christ is the head of the church, his body, of which he is the Savior. Now as the church submits to Christ, so also wives should submit to their husbands in everything.

"Husbands, love your wives, just as Christ loved the church and gave himself up for her to make her holy, cleansing her by the washing with water through the word, and to present her to himself as a radiant church, without stain or wrinkle or any other blemish, but holy and blameless. In this same way, husbands ought to love their wives as their own bodies. He who loves his wife loves himself. After all, no one ever hated his own body, but he feeds and cares for it, just as Christ does the church—for we are members of his body. 'For this reason a man will leave his father and mother and be united to his wife, and the two will become one flesh.' This is a profound mystery—but I am talking about Christ and the church. However, each one of you also must love his wife as he loves himself, and the wife must respect her husband."

—EPHESIANS 5:22-33

PRAYER

For him:

Lord, I love my wife with all of my heart, but I still find it difficult to express my love in ways that make her feel loved. Instead, I want to express my love in ways that make me feel loving, ways that make me feel good. Yet, that's not really love at all. It's selfish. Help me to be more sensitive, more in tune to her needs, and less concerned about my own.

For her:

Lord, I love and respect my husband, but I still find it difficult to submit to him in ways that make him feel fulfilled as a man. Help me to be more attentive to his needs and more responsive to his decisions.

In the name of Jesus l pray. Amen.

A MAN'S ROLE IN MARRIAGE: A LOVING LEADER[1]

According to the Scriptures, the roles for men and women in marriage are equal in value but different in function. It's critically important for a husband to understand this or he may be tempted to "lord" it over his wife. He is the head of his home, but that does not make him more important than his wife, just more responsible before God.

According to Ephesians 5, he is charged with the responsibility of providing both love and leadership. With these thoughts in mind, let's turn our attention to six principles of a loving leader.[2]

Principle # 1: Know your wife in order to look out for her welfare. You may be thinking that it's silly for me to even include so basic a principle. How could a man live with a woman without knowing her? Before you dismiss this principle out of hand, however, consider the following questions:

- What is your wife's greatest concern right now?
- What is her greatest need?
- What is her wildest dream?
- What is her smallest pain?
- What new vista would she like to explore?

If you cannot answer these questions with absolute certainty, then you probably don't know your wife as well as you think, and certainly not well enough to love her as you should.

Well-known author Madeleine L' Engle relates a story which illustrates what I am trying to say. "A Hasidic rabbi, renowned for his piety, was unexpectedly confronted one day by one of his devoted youthful disciples. In a burst of feeling, the young disciple exclaimed, 'My master, I love you!' The ancient teacher looked up from his books and asked his fervent disciple, 'Do you know what hurts me, my son?'

"The young man was puzzled. Composing himself, he stuttered, 'I don't understand your question, Rabbi. I am trying to tell you how much you mean to me, and you confuse me with irrelevant questions.'

"'My question is neither confusing nor irrelevant,' rejoined the rabbi, 'for if you do not know what hurts me, how can you truly love me?'"[3]

Principle # 2: Keep the channels of communication open and clear. Real communication can only flourish in an environment of love and trust. Your wife must feel safe with you before she will open up and share her whole heart. Only when she knows that you will really listen to her can she risk the depth of disclosure that produces true marital intimacy.

Principle # 3: Set an example. A loving leader models the behavior and values that he desires in his wife and children. For instance, if he wants his wife to share her heart with him, he must open his heart to her. When he practices being transparent and vulnerable, she will be encouraged to respond in kind. The same thing is true for respect, or kindness or even charity. A loving leader practices these virtues as a way of encouraging them in his wife and children.

Principle # 4: Make sound and timely decisions. A leader's primary responsibility is to lead, and that entails decision making. Unfortunately, there is an increasing number of men who are abdicating this vital responsibility. Some of it has to do with their personalities, but conditioning, I believe, plays a greater role. With the rise of the feminist movement, traditional roles for men have been called into question including decision making. As a result, many men are less sure of themselves, and this is reflected in their inability to make wise and timely decisions.

While this new submissiveness may be welcomed by today's feminist, it is a source of increasing frustration for the Christian woman. She wants her man to be the head of their home—not a tyrant or a dictator, but the loving leader described in Ephesians 5.

How, you may be thinking, *can an indecisive man learn to be decisive?* While there is no easy answer, there are some disciplines which, if practiced, will provide help and encouragement. In order to make wise and timely decisions, a man should seek the counsel of a trusted Christian brother. He should discuss the situation in depth with his wife, giving careful consideration to her input. Finally, he should ask God for special wisdom. "If any of you lacks wisdom, he should ask God, who gives generously to all without finding fault, and it will be given to him."[4]

Principle # 5: Determine your wife's gifts and capabilities and encourage her accordingly. The gifts and abilities your wife has were given to her by God. Therefore it is vitally important that you encourage your wife to maximize her God-given gifts. Not only will this benefit the Kingdom of God but the family as well, for a fulfilled woman will be a better wife and mother.

Principle # 6: Seek responsibility and take responsibility for your actions. When it's time to do the right thing, time to make tough decisions, it's time for the husband to step forward and assume responsibility. This is true whether it involves a tough parent-teacher conference, or a painful decision regarding the care of an aged parent. A wife shouldn't be expected to make those kinds of decisions alone, no matter how busy her husband is.

And when you make a mistake, be man enough to own it and do what you can to make restitution. I've never known anyone to bat a thousand in decision making, and you probably won't either. It's not important for you to be perfect, but it is critical that you recognize your mistakes and take responsibility for them.

ACTION STEPS

- Memorize the six principles of a loving leader:
  1) Know your wife in order to look out for her welfare.
  2) Keep the channels of communication open and clear.
  3) Set an example.
  4) Make sound and timely decisions.

5) Determine your wife's gifts and capabilities and encourage her accordingly.

6) Seek responsibility and take responsibility for your actions.

- On a scale of one to ten, with ten being a perfect score, rate yourself as a loving leader based on these six principles. Give yourself a one to ten rating for each one of the six principles.
- Now ask your wife to give you a one to ten rating on each one of the six principles. When she is finished, compare your scores. Ask her to suggest specific ways you can improve in these particular areas. Conclude with a time of prayer together.

THOUGHT FOR THE DAY

"Headship is leadership, a leadership of love. It is not a general commanding his army, a computer analyst pushing the right buttons, a master in charge of his slave. It is simply taking our God-given responsibility to care for our wives and families and to lead them in love toward the goals which God has chosen for us."[5]

—Jack Mayhall

"The image here is not that of a mighty potentate sitting on his throne, ruling his cowering subjects with an iron hand. This is more like a conductor standing on his box directing a symphony. Delicate, but definite! Subdued, yet powerful!"[6]

—Charlie W. Shedd

SCRIPTURE FOR THE DAY

"Two are better than one, because they have a good return for their work:
If one falls down, his friend can help him up.
But pity the man who falls and has no one to help him up!
Also, if two lie down together, they will keep warm. But how can one keep warm alone?

Though one may be overpowered, two can defend themselves.
A cord of three strands is not quickly broken."

—ECCLESIASTES 4:9-12

PRAYER

Lord, I am challenged by all that it means to be a Christian husband. I want to love my wife. I want to encourage her and affirm her I want to know her, I mean, really know her. I want to understand her so I can share her life. Yet, in the press of living I often become so engrossed in my other responsibilities that I neglect her, or I give her the leftovers of my time and attention. Forgive me, Lord. Help me to do better. Express Your eternal love through me. In the name of Jesus I pray. Amen.

AN IMPOSSIBLE TASK

"Who are you kidding?" he demanded. "There's not a man alive who could do all of that, no matter how hard he tried."

The speaker was slightly overweight and in his mid-thirties. Beside him, his wife seemed to shrink with embarrassment, but around the room several men nodded in agreement.

I was leading a marriage retreat, and it was obvious that I had touched a nerve. For the past few minutes we had been trying to write a job description for a Christian husband and father. Thus far we had twenty-nine entries, ranging from a servant leader to a compassionate companion to a father who gives priority time and attention to his children. Although our list was incomplete, it was readily obvious that there wasn't a man among us who could measure up.

Having done this very exercise at countless marriage retreats, I knew what to expect. It was only a matter of time until some overstressed husband protested the impossibility of it all. He would then be joined by a chorus of voices all agreeing with him. As if on cue, the heavyset husband gave voice to his growing agitation and was joined in protest by a majority of the men present.

Pausing, I let the undercurrent of comments subside, then I said, "You are absolutely right! There is not a man among us who can live up to the biblical model for a husband and father. It's an impossible task."

I let that sink in, then said, "We will never be the kind of husbands and fathers God has called us to be until we come to grips with that fact. Without the help of the Holy Spirit we will always fail, we will always fall short of this divine ideal. But with God's help we '...can do everything through him who gives [us] strength.'"[1]

As surely as we need God's help to overcome temptation, to master the disciplines of prayer and to mature as men of God, so we need divine enablement to become the kind of husbands and fathers our families need us to be. Even as God willingly helps us in all the other areas of our lives, so will He help us become godly husbands and fathers.

Picking up the list I began to read, "I can love my wife unconditionally and selflessly through Him who gives me strength."

"I can become my wife's best friend through Him who gives me strength."

"I can become a sensitive listener through Him who gives me strength."

"I can become the spiritual leader of my family through Him who gives me strength."

"I can put my wife and children's needs above my own through Him who gives me strength."

Many times we fail in our attempts to be godly husbands and fathers simply because we try to do it in our own strength. We know what is expected of us. We know the principles, the right things to do. Yet, in the moment of decision, we fail because we depend upon our own abilities rather than seeking God's help. At least, that has been my personal experience.

For years I struggled with irritability and impatience, especially toward Brenda. On many occasions I vowed to curb my tongue only to fall prey again to my carnal nature. To me it was no big deal, but for Brenda it was a continuing source of humiliation and pain.

Things finally came to a head, and I realized, maybe for the first time, what I was doing to Brenda. Momentarily, I felt hopeless. How many times had I vowed to change without success? Why should this time be different? Yet, I also knew that if things didn't change, our marriage was in trouble.

In desperation, I cried out to the Lord. I told Him that I was powerless to change myself. In prayer, I asked Him to set a watch over my lips. I asked Him to change my heart and my spirit, to make me a kind and gentle man.

Immediately, I noticed a change. I felt different on the inside, more relaxed, more peaceful. Things that had upset me in the past no longer upset me. Instead of lashing out at the slightest provocation, I now let things slide.

Every day for weeks I prayed that prayer. Sometimes I prayed it several times a day. Then I begin to take my new behavior for granted. I stopped asking God for help in that particular area. A few days later I caught myself lashing out at Brenda again.

Once more I was brought face-to-face with my human weakness and the resulting sinfulness. Taking Brenda's hand, I asked her to pray with me. Once more I acknowledged my weakness, my helplessness, and sought God's help. And again He graciously touched me.

I share all of that with you simply to encourage you to seek God's help in your own life and marriage. God has no favorites, and what He did for me He will do for you. In truth, you are also powerless to change, powerless to become what you know you ought to be. But with God all things are possible! And I am "...confident of this, that he who began a good work in you will carry it on to completion until the day of Christ Jesus."[2]

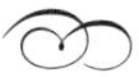

ACTION STEPS

- Make a list of the areas in which you fall short of the biblical model for a spouse and/or parent. Be specific.
- In prayer, confess your failures to God and ask Him to empower you to change. Pray specifically.
- Acknowledge your shortcomings to your spouse and ask him/her to agree with you in prayer.

THOUGHT FOR THE DAY

'True manhood calls for discipline of character, strong determination to set a course of action, and courage to stay at a task. But brutality? Vulgarity? Lack of courtesy? Hardly. Authentic men aren't afraid to show affection, release their feelings, hug their children, cry when they're sad, admit it when they're wrong, and ask for help when they need it. Vulnerability fits beautifully into mature manhood. So does integrity."[3]

—Charles R. Swindoll

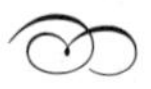

SCRIPTURE FOR THE DAY

"At that time Hanani the seer came to Asa king of Judah and said to him: 'Because you relied on the king of Aram and not on the Lord your God, the army of the king of Aram has escaped from your hand. Were not the Cushites and Libyans a mighty army with great numbers of chariots and horsemen? Yet when you relied on the Lord, he delivered them into your hand. For the eyes of the Lord range throughout the earth to strengthen those whose hearts are fully committed to him. You have done a foolish thing, and from now on you will be at war.'"

—2 CHRONICLES 16:7-9

PRAYER

Lord, I acknowledge my human limitations, the power of my carnal nature and my sinful failures as a husband and a father. I want to do better, but I seem powerless to change. In the past I have relied upon myself, and I have failed.

Beginning today I rely only upon You. You are my strength and my salvation. With Your enablement I will change, I will become the man, the husband, You have called me to be. In the name of Jesus I pray. Amen.

A WOMAN'S ROLE IN MARRIAGE: A SUPPORTIVE HELPMATE

Blessed indeed is the man who marries a woman wise enough to give him counsel and secure enough to allow him to be the leader in their home. Of her, the Scriptures declare, "...She is worth far more than rubies. Her husband has full confidence in her ... She brings him good, not harm, all the days of her life."[1]

Although she can do many things as well as her husband, and some even better than he, she willingly submits to him out of obedience to the Lord. She realizes that two captains sink the ship and two cooks spoil the broth; therefore, she honors her husband as the head of their family.

In the course of my work with couples, both as a pastor and a retreat leader, I have identified six things that characterize this kind of wife. Let's consider them one at a time.

1) She listens without giving advice. She realizes that there are times when her man needs a safe place where he can unburden his heart without fear of criticism or rejection. Furthermore, she knows, intuitively, that unsolicited advice feels like criticism.

Pity the man who is married to a woman who cannot listen without offering advice. Well might he plead:

"When I ask you to listen to me and you start giving me advice, you have not done what I asked.

"When I ask you to listen to me and you feel you have to do something to solve my problem, you have failed me, strange as that may seem.

"Listen! All I asked was that you listen, not talk or do—just hear me.

"Advice is cheap; 50 cents will get you both 'Dear Abby' and Billy Graham in the same paper.

"I can do for myself—I'm not helpless.

"When you do something for me that I can and need to do for myself, you contribute to my fear and inadequacy.

"But when you accept as a simple fact that I do feel what I feel, no matter how irrational, then I can quit trying to convince you and can get about this business of understanding what's behind this irrational feeling. When that's clear, the answers are obvious and I don't need advice.

"Nonrational feelings make more sense when we understand what's behind them.

"So please listen and just hear me.

"And if you want to talk, wait a minute for your turn—and I'll listen to you."

I suspect that the anonymous writer who penned those words was a husband married to a wordy but unwise wife.

2) She provides wise counsel. "She speaks with wisdom, and faithful instruction is on her tongue."[2] Even as she knows when to listen and not speak, so she also knows that there are times when her husband needs and desires her counsel. There are times when he trusts her guidance above all others. Not just because she is wise, but because he knows that she desires his success as she desires her own.

3) She supports her husband's decisions. This is a relatively easy thing for her to do when they have come to a mutual understanding. It is, however, an altogether different matter when he makes a decision that she feels is unwise. Still, the time for discussion and advice is past. Now she must lay aside her concerns and support her husband's decision.

Paul begins his instructions to husbands and wives in Ephesians 5 by encouraging them to "submit to one another out of reverence for Christ."[3] With these words he establishes the framework for godly decision making. If both the husband

and the wife are totally submitted to Christ, and if they are both fully seeking His will, it only stands to reason that they will come to the same decision.

Unfortunately, in real life, even committed Christians sometimes allow their own desires to cloud the clear direction of the Holy Spirit. When that happens in a marriage, a couple is likely to find themselves at odds over important decisions.

For this reason God has provided a biblical model for resolving the impasse: "Wives, submit to your husbands as to the Lord."[4]

As Dr. James Dobson says, "...a family must have a leader whose decisions prevail in times of differing opinions."[5] He goes on to say, "If I understand the Scriptures, that role has been assigned to the man of the house. However, he must not incite his crew to mutiny by heavy-handed disregard for their feelings and needs. He should, in fact, put the best interests of his family above his own, even to the point of death if necessary. Nowhere in Scripture is he authorized to become a dictator or slave-owner."[6]

4) She honors his need for personal time. No matter how much a husband loves his wife, regardless of how compatible they are, he still needs some time just for himself. If his wife is insecure, she may interpret his need for solitude as rejection, and thus feel hurt. If she spends all day with their preschool age children, she may feel that his need for solitude is selfish and insensitive, and thus resent it. But if she can realize that his need for solitude is truly a manifestation of the way God created him, then she can give him his personal time as a gift of her love.

How much solitude he requires and when he takes it are details that need to be worked out between the spouses. Retreating to the bedroom to read the paper or to watch the evening news immediately upon arriving home in the evening probably isn't a good idea if his wife has spent all day alone with the children. On the other hand, if both spouses work outside the home, a few minutes of solitude immediately upon arriving home may be just what the doctor ordered.

While the need for solitude is universal, the way it is worked out in marriage will vary from couple to couple. The important thing to remember is that personal space enhances marital intimacy rather than detracting from it. And it is a wise woman who honors her husband's need for personal time.

5) She affirms his manhood, especially during stressful times. A high school teacher and his wife went to see their pastor for counseling. During one of the sessions his wife said that she always made love with her husband on payday. Taking the bait, her pastor asked, "Why?"

"My husband's a very good teacher," she explained, "but it seems he is tempted to give up teaching at least once a month—on payday. He deposits our check in the bank and then comes home and spends the evening writing out checks to pay our bills. By the time he has paid the mortgage payment on the house, our car payment, his school loans, the utility bills, and given me the grocery allowance for the month there's nothing left. He feels like a failure then, especially when he compares his meager salary to what some of his classmates earn who went into business or law.

"I tried telling him what a good teacher he is, what a difference he is making in the lives of young people, even how proud I am of what he is doing, but nothing worked. He would mope around the house for days.

"One day I was telling my mother about it when she laughed. 'Honey,' she said, 'when your daddy gets like that I just take him to the bedroom and make love to him. It works every time.'

"And pastor," she concluded, "Mom was right. It works every time."

The pastor risked a glance at her husband. He looked a little embarrassed, but there was also a gleam in his eye when he looked at his wife.

I don't mean to suggest that every problem your husband has can be solved in the bedroom, but I do know that he will be better equipped to deal with the world if he can be assured of your love and respect. When he feels like a man, he is better able to make manly decisions.

6) She prays for her husband. Nothing she does is more important than this. Her prayers provide the covering that protects him from the snares of the enemy. Her prayers enable her to connect with him even when they are separated by time and distance. They give her insight and understanding into the unique needs he has, thus she is better able to minister to him. Her prayers contribute to the spiritual environment of their marriage, thus making it conducive for him to become the man God has called him to be.

ACTION STEPS

- Memorize the six characteristics of a godly wife.
  1) She listens without giving advice.
  2) She provides wise counsel.
  3) She supports her husband's decisions.
  4) She honors his need for personal time.
  5) She affirms his manhood, especially during stressful times.
  6) She prays for her husband.
- On a scale of one to ten, with ten being a perfect score, rate yourself as a supportive helpmate based on these six principles. Give yourself a one to ten rating for each one of the six principles.
- Now ask your husband to give you a one to ten rating on each one of the six principles. When he is finished, compare your scores. Ask him to suggest specific ways you can improve in these particular areas. Conclude with a time of prayer together.

THOUGHT FOR THE DAY

"What your husband needs will be a reflection of his longing for *companionship, intimacy,* and *significance.* How his needs will be demonstrated will be unique because he is unique. That is why, as a wife, you must make it your project to study your man. Where do you begin?

"Begin by asking God. Psalm 139 declares that God understands your man's thoughts, is intimately acquainted with all his ways. The Lord is the One who can teach you all you need to know about your man. He, our Creator, was there when your man was formed and placed in his mother's womb.

"Countless times I have gone to the Lord with this PRAYER: 'Help, God. Teach me to understand this complicated man You have given me to love.' Time after time, He has unraveled puzzles that I couldn't solve. Sometimes this insight has been given as I have been quiet before Him, other times through His Word or a book or the words of a friend."[7]

—Linda Dillow

SCRIPTURE FOR THE DAY

"Her children arise and call her blessed; her husband also, and he praises her;
'Many women do noble things, but you surpass them all.'
Charm is deceptive, and beauty is fleeting; but a woman who fears the Lord is to be praised.
Give her the reward she has earned, and let her works bring her praise at the city gate."

—PROVERBS 31:28-31

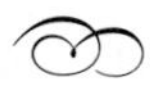

PRAYER

Lord, I am just an ordinary woman. I can't possibly do all of those things. I have children to raise, a home to keep and meals to cook. Yet, I want to be that kind of wife. Help me, Lord, for I feel overwhelmed. In the name of Jesus I pray. Amen.

THREE

COMMUNICATION—THE KEY TO MARRIAGE

SECTION 3

Communication—The Key to Marriage

"It fascinates me how differently we all speak in different circumstances. There are very formal occasions, often requiring written English: the job application or the letter to the editor—the dark-suit, serious-tie language, with everything pressed and the lint brushed off. There is our less formal out-in-the-world language—a more comfortable suit, but still respectable. There is language for close friends on weekends—blue-jeans and sweat-shirt language. There is family language, even more relaxed, full of grammatical shortcuts, family slang, echoes of old jokes that have become intimate shorthand—the language of pajamas and uncombed hair. Finally, there is the language with no clothes on; the talk of couples—murmurs, sighs—open and vulnerable language, at its least self-conscious."[1]

—Robert MacNeil

THE GENDER GAP

By vocation I am a communicator. Words are the tools of my trade. For nearly twenty-five years I was a pastor, and each week I preached at least three sermons, spent many hours in personal counseling and hosted a live call-in radio program. In addition, I am an author, having written thirty books and hundreds of articles. Yet, in my own marriage, meaningful communication is a constant challenge.

Why, you may be wondering, would a wordsmith like me be plagued with the same communication difficulties that are common to most couples? The first clue can be found in the dynamics of communication itself. According to the experts, words only play a small part in the art of communication—7 percent to be exact. Thirty-five percent of the message comes from our tone of voice, and the remaining 58 percent of the message is communicated through our body language—eye contact, facial expressions, etc. In other words, being gifted with words does not necessarily translate into effective marital communication.

Another factor is the fact that Brenda and I, like most men and women, speak a different language. Dr. Deborah Tannen, author of *You Just Don't Understand: Women and Men in Conversation,* says, "...boys and girls grow up speaking different languages and continue to do so as adults...for girls talk is a way in which intimacy is maintained. A little girl typically has a best friend, and they sit inside and tell each other secrets. And when girls play in groups they tend to make suggestions, rather than give orders, and the suggestions tend to be taken up and tend to be for the good of the group.

"For boys, who are likely to play in larger groups, it is the activity that is central. There are winners and losers, and the groups have a hierarchy. The high-status boys give orders and push the low-status boys around."[2]

As a rule, women tend to be relational, while men tend to be competitive, and the way they communicate reflects these differences. She wants to express her feelings in order to develop an intimate relationship. He wants to tell her why she shouldn't feel the way she feels. Though they both speak English, hers is the language of feelings while his is the language of power.

Now add to all of this the dynamics of the relationship itself—past failures, little hurts and not so little hurts, disappointments, unresolved conflicts, resentments—and it is not hard to understand why couples find it hard to communicate.

In our case, there was at least one additional factor. Brenda found my verbal skills intimidating. Not because she was a poor communicator, but because I had been very confrontive in the past. Instead of using my communication skills to affirm her and to encourage her to express herself, I had, too often, been judgmental and controlling. Since Brenda couldn't outtalk me, she resorted to her most effective tactic—silence.

When communication is lost, the heart and soul go out of your marriage. You experience a loneliness of the most haunting kind. You live in the same house, share the same bed, parent the same children, even make "love," yet you never really touch each other. For all the things you appear to have in common, you have become strangers.

Is there a solution, a way to bridge the gender gap, a way to develop meaningful communication in marriage? Absolutely! But like most tasks in the making of a marriage, it is hard work. Only the most determined couples truly learn to communicate; the rest settle for mediocrity.

ACTION STEPS

- Since meaningful communication engenders intimacy in marriage, an evaluation of the quality of marital intimacy can often give insight into a couple's level of communication. With that in mind, circle the number on the scales that follow that best indicates your feelings about the amount of intimacy you presently have in each dimension of your relationship.

Little Intimacy				**Much Intimacy**

a) Emotional: sharing feelings

I	2	3	4	5

b) Recreational: sharing leisure-time activities

I	2	3	4	5

c) Spiritual: sharing a sense of God and His presence

I	2	3	4	5

d) Sensual: sharing caresses and moments of tenderness

I	2	3	4	5

e) Sexual: sharing openness in sexual expression

I	2	3	4	5

f) Aesthetic: sharing a sense of beauty and wonder

I	2	3	4	5

g) Intellectual: sharing ideas and thoughts

I	2	3	4	5

- Discuss your ratings with your husband/wife.
- Plan two specific steps by which at least one area of intimacy can be met more fully.

THOUGHT FOR THE DAY

"If we want to be heard we must speak in a language the listener can understand and on a level at which the listener is capable of operating."[3]

—M. Scott Peck, M.D.

SCRIPTURE FOR THE DAY

"Reckless words pierce like a sword, but the tongue of the wise brings healing."

—PROVERBS 12:18

PRAYER

Lord, sometimes my words interfere with my ability to communicate. Rather than revealing my heart, they become a smoke screen obscuring my true feelings. Or I use my facility with words to overpower my spouse, and once again intimacy falls prey to my need to be right. Forgive me, Lord. I have not set a watch over my lips, therefore my gift with words has become a curse. Well did Oswald Chambers say, "An unguarded strength is a double weakness." Give me the tongue of the wise, l pray, that my words may heal those I have wounded. In Jesus' name I pray. Amen.

THE PERFECTIONIST

"The color is not right," she said. "It should be a different shade of purple."

Slamming on the brakes, I skidded to a stop. "Give it to me!" I ordered.

Without a word she handed the brochure to me. Angrily I wadded it up, before opening my door and flinging it into the street. "If the thing is that bad, let's just throw it out," I muttered, through clinched teeth.

Anger hung heavy between us, and we drove in silence for several miles. Already remorse was making me regret my angry outburst, but pride demanded I make no apology. Besides, Brenda was always finding fault. Don't misunderstand me, she is not a critical person, nor is she a nag. She is, however, a perfectionist of the first order. When she looks at anything, her eye is immediately drawn to any flaw it might have, even the slightest imperfection. It's a family trait, one that she inherited from her father.

Turning into our driveway, I pushed the button on the garage door opener and waited impatiently for the door to open. After pulling into the garage, I shut off the car engine, and we sat silently. Finally Brenda spoke. "I didn't mean to make you mad. I had no idea you would take my remarks personally."

"I overreacted," I acknowledged, "but it seems you are always doing that to me. I share something with you, and the first thing you do is point out the imperfections. You never just say, 'That's great,' or, 'I'm so happy for you,' or anything like that. It's always, 'The color is not quite right,' or, 'The lettering is wrong,' or something like that. Just once I would like to hear you say what you like about whatever I show you."

Brenda sat in thoughtful silence for a minute or two, then she said, "I want to change, I really do, but you will have to help me."

"How?" I asked.

"Instead of asking me what I think about something, ask me what I like best about it. When you do that," she explained, "you help me to focus on what I like, rather than the imperfections."

That incident took place several years ago, and I can report that we are doing much better. With my help Brenda is responding more positively. And when she does revert to her perfectionism, I try not to take it personally. As a consequence, I am less inclined to react in anger.

We might still be at each other's throat, however, had we not recognized our individual communication styles and deliberately set about to help each other communicate better. Brenda will always be a perfectionist, that's who she is, and I am an irrepressible fixer. By accepting the unchangeable and working with it, we have turned our differences into assets instead of liabilities. Although these differences present communication challenges, in other areas they are a real asset to the effective functioning of our family.

For instance, because Brenda is such a perfectionist, she is, by far, the better shopper in our family. Whether we are talking about clothes, or appliances, or cars or even a house, Brenda does the shopping. With her attention to detail, she notices things I would never see. And because she is a perfectionist, she never buys anything until she has found both the best product and the best bargain!

Because I am a problem-solver, I am able to see a number of possible solutions in situations where Brenda is stumped. Whether we are talking about a family problem, a financial concern or a relational difficulty, I can find an answer where Brenda is sure there is none to be found. Many a time she has been able to resolve a sticky situation by applying a principle that I provided. Working together, we make quite a team.

One of my favorite Peanuts cartoons shows Linus lying in front of the television watching a show. Lucy walks in, takes one look at the television screen and turns up her nose. Grabbing the remote control from Linus, she flips through the channels until she finds something she wants to watch.

Once she's comfortably ensconced in an easy chair, Linus turns to her and asks, "What makes you think you can walk in here and change the channel when I am in the middle of a program?"

Glancing at him disdainfully, she holds up her right hand. "Do you see these five fingers?" she asks. "Well, when they are tightly closed they form a formidable fist."

Without another word Lucy turns her attention back to the television. Bewildered, Linus looks at his own right hand with its five fingers and asks, "Why can't you guys get organized like that?"

When a husband and wife simply go their own way, they are like Linus' right hand. All the fingers are there, but that's about all that can be said. However, when they see their individual differences as mutually beneficial, and work together for their common good, they become "a formidable fist."

ACTION STEPS

- Identify your own communication style. What strengths and weaknesses are inherent in it?
- Identify your spouse's communication style. What strengths and weaknesses are inherent in it?
- Discuss some ways to help each other communicate more effectively. Be specific and stay focused on positive ways to help one another.
- Determine that you will work together to make your differences an asset instead of a liability.

THOUGHT FOR THE DAY

"It is not easy for us to change. But it is possible. And it is our glory as human beings."[1]

—M. Scott Peck, M.D.

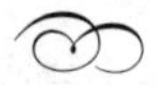

SCRIPTURE FOR THE DAY

"The wisdom of the prudent is to give thought to their ways, but the folly of fools is deception."

—PROVERBS 14:8

PRAYER

Lord, the willingness to change is a rare quality indeed. I am so thankful that You allowed me to marry a person who is willing to do so. I must confess that change isn't easy for me. When someone suggests it, I become defensive, even argumentative. Forgive me, Lord, and help me to be willing to change. In the name of Jesus I pray. Amen.

THE IRREPRESSIBLE FIXER

For years I frustrated Brenda with advice and exhortations. When she shared a problem or concern with me, I always had a ready answer. The things that troubled her seemed so insignificant to me, so easy to solve. Unfortunately, it was not my "wisdom" she sought, but my understanding. Not realizing this, I continued to advise her until she finally stopped discussing her concerns with me. I was a "fixer," and she needed a compassionate husband who would simply accept her and listen with love.

Needless to say, my insensitivity took its toll. She stopped sharing her needs and concerns, but I hardly noticed, so busy was I in my own world. My easy answers and constant advice had only made her feel silly and inadequate. And angry, I might add, so she suffered alone with her hurt. Over the years this situation, plus the never-ending demands of the ministry, took their toll, and Brenda grew depressed. She was careful to hide her feelings from me. I had not proved worthy of her trust.

Thankfully, Jesus was doing His special work in my heart, and as I came to understand myself, I was gradually being changed, being prepared to be a truly godly husband.

One winter evening I came home early and found Brenda in the bedroom crying. When she heard my step on the stairs, she tried to dry her tears, but it was too late. With great trepidation she poured out her hurts and fears, her self-doubts.

For once I listened, with compassion, and didn't try to "fix" everything. Her pain and aloneness became mine. I understood. We sat for a long time that night, after her grief had spent itself, in loving silence.

This time there was no advice or exhortation to do better. I simply loved her and accepted her in her need. On the inside I grieved, for I knew that her pain and aloneness were, at least partially, my fault. If I had been more compassionate, more understanding… If I had been the kind of husband I should have been… With a determined effort I refused to allow my guilt to get in the way of her need. This was Brenda's time, and I chose to be there for her.

Brenda wasn't suddenly free from her lonely depression, but she began to believe that I might be able to understand her. Bit by bit she began to trust me with her feelings again. And, as I continued to respond with compassion and understanding, the depth of our communication deepened.

ACTION STEPS

- Think back over some of your recent conversations with your spouse. Have you been willing to listen without offering advice? Ask your spouse if you are a good listener.
- Ask your spouse to help you become a compassionate listener. Give him/her permission to begin a conversation by saying something like: "I am not asking for advice or suggestions right now. I just need for you to listen to me and to try to understand what I am feeling."
- Agree together in prayer, asking God to help both of you become compassionate listeners.

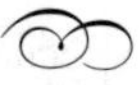

THOUGHT FOR THE DAY

"No one can develop freely in this world and find a full life without feeling understood by at least one person. Misunderstood, he loses his self-confidence, he loses his faith in life or even in God. He is blocked and he regresses."[1]

"It is thus vain to hope to understand one's husband or wife without listening long, and with great interest.… The essential part … is listening, long and passionate listening, with love and respect and with a real effort at understanding."[2]

—Paul Tournier

SCRIPTURE FOR THE DAY

"Do not be quick with your mouth, do not be hasty in your heart to utter anything before God.

God is in heaven and you are on earth, so let your words be few.

As a dream comes when there are many cares, so the speech of a fool when there are many words."

—ECCLESIASTES 5:2,3

PRAYER

Lord, give me ears to hear, a heart to understand, a will to respond and compassion to make my response merciful and loving. In the name of Jesus I pray. Amen.

CULTIVATING CLOSENESS

According to the Scriptures, God intends for marriage to be a special relationship in which two people truly become one, experiencing the deepest intimacy and the most complete fulfillment of which they are capable. "For this reason a man will leave his father and mother and be united to his wife, *and they will become one flesh*"[1] (italics mine).

Dr. Desmond Morris describes the experience of becoming one as bonding. It "...refers to the emotional covenant that links a man and woman together for life. It is the specialness which sets those two lovers apart from every other person on the face of the earth."[2]

At the beginning, this blessed oneness is embryonic. That is, it is true in the spirit of their marriage, but not in the reality of their day-to-day lives. Two separate and distinct people are not suddenly one simply because a minister pronounces them husband and wife. They *become* one flesh. It takes time and commitment, not to mention love and hard work.

Unfortunately, few couples ever experience this level of intimacy. They simply do not communicate on a level that makes this type of bonding possible. They talk, but only on a surface level. He doesn't know how to express his innermost thoughts and feelings. In truth, he's more than a little afraid of them. Consequently, he has never allowed himself to get in touch with his inner self. Tragically, he is a stranger, not only to his wife, but to himself as well.

She is more conscious of her inner self, but no more able to share than he is. Her reasons are different, but no less inhibiting. What if she were to disclose some deeply intimate experience only to have him respond with indifference. That's a possibility she simply cannot face. She tried to share on that level once, shortly after they were married, and he just looked at her, not comprehending. The emotional isolation she felt in that moment was unbearable. She cannot risk it again.

Yet, for the couple who dares to plumb the depths of their thoughts and feelings, there remains an intimacy that can only be described as a blessed oneness. This is the ultimate achievement of marriage—the merging of self into self until there can never be one without the other. Yet in their oneness they have lost nothing of their individual personality. In fact, because of the security of their oneness, each of them is more their individual self than they have ever been. Freed from the fear of misunderstanding or rejection, they can truly be the self God meant them to be.

Where love is carefully nurtured, communication can be cultivated, and this blessed oneness can be achieved. Because she loves him completely, he can trust her with his life. He tells her his hidden fears, the secret doubts he has never dared share with anyone. In her presence, in the circle of her love, nothing he thinks or says seems insignificant or foolish.

And as he tells her his whole heart, not all at once, but over an extended period, they become one. She takes his life into her own. His joy is now hers. His childhood and adolescence are now part of her past too. His pain is hers as well, and his victories, his achievements, become theirs—the "stuff' of which their oneness is made.

Because he loves her completely, selflessly, she can trust him with her heart. In the quiet of evening, after the children have been put to bed, she tells him the story of her life. Not just the past with its memories, both good and bad, but the events of her day as well. The phone call she received from an old friend, the gist of the conversation she shared with a neighbor over coffee, something one of the children did. Little things, insignificant taken alone, but together they are the fabric of her life. And in the sharing, they become part of his life as well. They become their life—their oneness.

This is the goal of communication. This is the meaning of marriage.

ACTION STEPS

- How much time have you spent in interaction with your husband/wife this week?

  a) _____ less than 15 minutes daily

  b) _____ 15-20 minutes daily

  c) _____ 30-60 minutes daily

  d) _____ more than 60 minutes daily

  e) _____ other (write in the amount of time)

- Write one or two words that best characterize the interaction you had (e.g., tense, fun, meaningful).
- What activities have you shared with each other this week?
- How would you characterize the nature of the time and activities spent with each other (e.g., performing household tasks, problem solving, worship, leisure time activities, etc.)?
- Is this the kind of interaction that will enable you to reach the level of sharing that will make it possible for you to truly bond with one another? If not, what changes do you need to make to cultivate that kind of sharing with one another?

THOUGHT FOR THE DAY

"Deep sharing is overwhelming, and very rare. A thousand fears keep us in check. First of all, there is the fear of breaking down, of crying. There is especially the fear that the other will not sense the tremendous importance with which this memory or feeling is charged. How painful it is when such a difficult sharing falls flat, upon ears either preoccupied or mocking, ears in any case that do not sense the significance of what we're saying.

"It may happen between man and wife. The partner who has thus spoken in a very personal way without being understood falls back into a terrible emotional solitude."[3]

—Paul Tournier

SCRIPTURE FOR THE DAY

"May the God who gives endurance and encouragement give you a spirit of unity among yourselves as you follow Christ Jesus, so that with one heart and mouth you may glorify the God and Father of our Lord Jesus Christ.

"Accept one another, then, just as Christ accepted you, in order to bring praise to God…

"May the God of hope fill you with all joy and peace as you trust in him, so that you may overflow with hope by the power of the Holy Spirit."

—ROMANS 15:5-7,13

PRAYER

Lord, enable me to love my spouse in such a way that he/she feels secure enough to share his/her innermost thoughts and feelings. Grant me understanding that I may treat his/her gift of self with respect. Give me the courage that I may respond in kind, that I, too, may share my most private self. And as a result of our vulnerable transparency, may we truly become one. In the name of Jesus I pray. Amen.

THE MUSIC OF MARRIAGE

Probably more marriages end in divorce as a result of a breakdown in communication than for any other single cause. Therefore it is critically important that you and your spouse keep the lines of communication open between you at all costs. When you stop communicating with each other, you begin to drift apart, walls are erected between you and resentments build.

Many newlywed couples mistakenly assume that communication will take care of itself. During courtship they talked for hours and hours, why should marriage change that? Maybe it shouldn't, but it often does. According to author and marriage counselor H. Norman Wright, "...when a couple enters marriage, each person is demanding little but receiving much. Under the influence of very intense feelings, each responds to the other's needs. But in time this changes. More demands are now made on each of them from the outside, whereas previously most of the attention could be focused on their partner. As outside demands increase, we tend to meet less of our spouse's needs in order to fulfill more of our own needs. The couple moves into the stage of giving less and expecting more and unfulfilled needs become a source of conflict."[1]

My experience, both as a husband and as a pastor working with couples, tends to bear him out. Meaningful communication takes time and energy. When both spouses work outside the home, they often have little time, and even less energy, to invest in their relationship. Add the demands of parenting, when children enter the picture, and it is not hard to see why couples talk less and less. While they are communicating less, their need for the closeness, which comes as a result of deep sharing, is not diminished. The frustration of this need for emotional intimacy often becomes a source of anger, or even resentment.

How a couple handles the resulting conflict will determine, to a significant degree, the quality of their marriage. If they acknowledge what's happening, and take steps to give priority time and energy to their relationship, they can move to a new level of communication. Whereas, during courtship, their communication was based on intensely romantic feelings, it is now based on commitment, an act of their will.

One way that Brenda and I maintain communication is to go to bed together each night. This requires a commitment. Some evenings it means I will miss a late-night sporting event. On other occasions, Brenda will choose to come to bed with me rather than stay up to watch a movie with our daughter. Although there are times when one of us really would like to do something else, we are both committed to this time together. Knowing that we have an appointed time for connecting with each other allows us to pursue our individual responsibilities without fear of drifting apart.

Once we are both in bed, we spend a few minutes "checking in"—catching up on our day, sharing plans for tomorrow or the coming weekend. This is not a time for dealing with heavy issues or resolving conflict. Rather, it is a time when we simply open our hearts to one another. After a while we join hands and share a time of prayer. Then we give ourselves to sleep, secure in the knowledge that we are one.

It is not mandatory that your commitment to meaningful communication be exactly like ours, or anyone else's for that matter. What is important is that you agree together on a regular time and place for the kind of in-depth sharing that renews your marriage. Indeed, it may be the very thing that sustains your marriage in the time of crisis.

Communication is an art, and like any art form it requires disciplined practice. Initially, the practice may be tedious and unfulfilling. Many people drop out or look for shortcuts, but those who stick with it are rewarded with deep and fulfilling relationships. Like a musician who has mastered his instrument, they are free to make beautiful music—and communication is the music of marriage.

ACTION STEPS

- With your spouse discuss ways of improving your communication. Be specific.
- Now agree together on an appointed time and place when you will "connect" with each other on a regular basis—daily or at least weekly.

THOUGHT FOR THE DAY

"Anne Philipe gives a vivid picture of the normal fluctuations in the depth and intensity of intimacy, and of the periodic renewal of significant communication which revivifies a good marriage:

"'The inhuman city rhythm would sometimes separate us for several days.... In, out, telephones, sleep. For a while the communication would be broken, the light between us dimmed, but we knew that the next Sunday would see us reunited and we would tell each other then all that the interminable week had brought to us both: thoughts about ourselves, things we had heard, things we had observed each in the other without seeming to, as we had seemed absorbed. I like it when you noticed my new sweater after you hadn't said a word about it the morning I put it on for the first time.'"[2]

—Howard and Charlotte Clinebell

SCRIPTURE FOR THE DAY

"But Ruth replied, 'Don't urge me to leave you or to turn back from you. Where you go I will go, and where you stay I will stay. Your people will be my people and your God my God. Where you die I will die, and there I will be buried. May the Lord deal with me, be it ever so severely, if anything but death separates you and me.'"

—RUTH 1:16,17

PRAYER

Lord, there are times when I simply don't want to communicate. I don't want to share my deepest feelings, nor do I want to be burdened with those of my spouse. Yet, when I withdraw, when I isolate myself, I ache with loneliness. I am tempted to pray, "Take this loneliness from me," but instead I pray, "Let this loneliness drive me to my beloved. And in deep sharing may we find the intimacy that makes us one." In the name of Jesus l pray. Amen.

FOUR

Love and Anger

SECTION 4

LOVE AND ANGER

"A relationship which spells closeness also spells conflict. Some conflict, unhappiness, frustration, and anger are inherent and inescapable in every marriage relationship simply because they are in the fabric of all human relationships. Marriage is like other human relationships, only more so. That is, marriage is the most difficult and the most demanding, but also the most potentially rewarding of all human relationships, because it is potentially the most intimate. Because it is the most intimate, it also holds the greatest potential for conflict.

"Conflict in itself is not a block to intimacy. People who feel strongly about each other are bound to fight occasionally.... A couple can learn to learn from their fights; they can learn how to keep them from becoming physically or emotionally destructive, how to interrupt them sooner and how to grow closer because of them. Intimacy grows when conflicts are faced and worked through in the painful but fulfilling process of gradual understanding and compromise of differences."[1]

—Howard & Charlotte Clinebell

COUPLES IN CONFLICT

Four out of every ten marriages in the United States end in divorce before the seventh anniversary. That means that annually about two-and-a-half million men and women will petition for the dissolution of their marriage. Add to these grim statistics the fact that most marriages that fail never reach the divorce court, and you have a tragedy of immense proportion.

Some couples make peace with their pain; they give up their dreams and live out their lives in mediocrity. They are together, but not intimate. Others live in a kind of "cold war." They tolerate each other, but barely, and never miss an opportunity to let their dissatisfaction be known. Divorce is out of the question, but so is love. He has mastered the unholy art of saying, "Yes, dear," in a way that clearly says she is not dear to him! For her part, she has perfected a contemptuous glance, accompanied by a certain pursing of her lips, that can stop him dead in his tracks, across a room full of people.

Then there are those couples who quarrel bitterly. Their marriage is a combat zone; verbal and emotional abuse is the order of the day. Angry words leave their fragile self-images sorely wounded. Finally, there are the martyrs, those sad souls who suffer in silence, who have made a lifelong pact with self-pity. Misery is the one thing all these couples have in common—and anger.

Surely there must be a better way; some way of transcending differences, some way of releasing hurts and anger, some way of resolving conflicts. There is, but it won't be easy and everything within will fight against it. When your marriage fails to live up to your expectations, you naturally tend to blame your spouse. Instead, you must accept your share of the responsibility and determine that you will change. You will be tempted to excuse yourself, to justify your shortcomings as simply being the way you are. That may appear true to you, but it is not true; at least it is not totally true.

The real reason we sin against our marriages goes much deeper than our personal idiosyncrasies. At the very core of our being we are self-centered, selfish, and determined to have our own way no matter what the cost. And selfishness, as we all know, is the original sin. Adam and Eve selfishly insisted on doing things their way rather than God's way. This same spirit is at work in all of us, undermining, not only our marriages, but all the relationships of our lives. That is both our damnation and our salvation. Our damnation because sin always steals and destroys. Our salvation because sin can be forgiven, and the sinner can be changed!

If we claim that our behavior is fated, or if we explain it as a quirk of our personality, that it's "just the way we are," then our situation is hopeless. Personalities, as any counselor knows, are almost impossible to change. On the other hand, to admit that our marital failures are rooted in sin invites the power of God into our situation. And God can eradicate sin and transform the sinner.

ACTION STEPS

- If you are experiencing ongoing conflict in your marriage, ask God to show you where you are at fault.
- If the source of your marital conflict is rooted in long-standing habits and behaviors, get professional help. Be willing to seek marital counseling, especially if your spouse requests it.

THOUGHT FOR THE DAY

"I was a fool in those days. I did not see that even my efforts at healing hurt her. Well, I wasn't looking at these present efforts, only at past actions to find the fault; but, in fact, the fault was consistently there, in me, in all that I was doing. Therefore, I kept making things worse for all my good intentions. I was a walking fault!"[2]

"I knew for sure that Thanne was right. I had sinned terribly against her, sins which I will name before this chapter is done, so you will understand that it wasn't a single act or a number of acts: it was I myself. I was sin."[3]

—Walter Wangerin, Jr.

SCRIPTURE FOR THE DAY

"Search me, O God, and know my heart; test me and know my anxious thoughts.
See if there is any offensive way in me, and lead me in the way everlasting."

—PSALM 139:23,24

PRAYER

Lord Jesus, I have sinned against my marriage. I have sinned out of ignorance and insensitivity, not knowing what I was doing. I have sinned out of anger, spitefully, returning hurt for hurt. I have sinned premeditatedly, selfishly seeking my own pleasure, without considering the consequences. Forgive me, Lord Jesus. Transform me. Make me a new person, a godly person. Restore my marriage, and heal all the hurts I have caused. In Your holy name I pray. Amen.

HELP, I'M ANGRY!

David Mace world-renowned marriage and family counselor, writes in *Love and Anger in Marriage,* "The state of marriage generates in normal people more anger than they are likely to experience in any other type of relationship in which they habitually find themselves."[1]

If he's right, and I believe he is, then we need to ask ourselves why. Why does marriage, which is potentially the most intimate of all relationships, generate so much anger? Remember, Mace is not talking about dysfunctional marriages. If he were, his statement would be self-explanatory. I mean, it is no mystery why a betrayed spouse feels angry, or why the wife of an alcoholic finds herself in a rage. No, the question before us is, why does a relatively good marriage generate so much anger?

I think there are at least two reasons, both of which say something positive about the relationship. First, we care more about our marriage than we do about any other relationship in our life. We care what other people do, but only up to a point. Because they are not a permanent part of our life, their actions have no lasting effect upon us, and we seldom allow them to make us angry. In marriage, things are different. What our spouse does, what he/she feels, or thinks, has a direct bearing upon our own well-being. It is accurate, I believe, to say that the amount of anger we feel is often in direct proportion to how much we care.

The second reason deals more with why we express anger in marriage, rather than why marriage generates anger in us. We express anger within the confines of our marriage because we feel safe there. We know that we can say things to our spouse that we could never say to our boss, or even a friend. Our spouse may become angry with us, may even fight back, but when the anger has passed we will still be loved and accepted.

According to Howard and Charlotte Clinebell, authors of *The Intimate Marriage*, "Occasional outbursts may make it possible for the marriage partners to be more caring and compassionate at other times. A relationship strong enough to take such outbursts in its stride is a healthy one. Providing a place where one can safely drain off hostility that has accumulated in the outside world is one of the important mental health functions of a good marriage."[2] They go on to point out, however, "Chronic verbal attacking is not a means of maintaining a healthy marriage."[3]

Having identified at least two positive attributes of anger in marriage, let me hasten to add that I am not encouraging indiscriminate outbursts. As a child I used to sing, "Sticks and stones may break my bones, but words can never hurt me." Now I know better—"Reckless words pierce like a sword...."[4] Many an angry spouse has sorely wounded the very one he/she loves.

Since anger is an inevitable part of marriage, it is important that we develop healthy ways of dealing with it. Remember, it is a powerful emotion and should be handled with care.

There are three basic ways of dealing with anger. First, there is the world's way: *Express it*—let it all hang out! Let the chips fall where they may. The repercussions of such a response should be obvious. Express your anger indiscriminately, and the people you care most about are going to get hurt. As a minister, I've witnessed the consequences of this flawed strategy on numerous occasions. I've intervened in family fights, rescued abused children and comforted battered wives. And I've heard the sobbing confessions of remorseful men, once their anger was spent.

The second way is the Church's way: *Repress it*—deny your feelings! Pretend that you are not angry at all. People who handle their anger by repressing it subsequently suffer any number of physical and psychological symptoms. When a person feels strong negative emotions, his bodily functions change. His bladder and colon tend to empty. His blood pressure rises. Adrenaline, a substance that provides energy, is produced in much greater quantity. Muscles tighten, saliva dries up. If he bottles up those feelings for very long, he will probably experience some type of psychosomatic illness, ranging from a spastic colon, an ulcer, a rash or even a heart attack.

You are probably asking, "What am I supposed to do? If I ventilate my anger, let it all hang out, it's destructive. People get hurt, things get broken. If I repress it, if I hold it in, I run the risk of becoming depressed or physically ill. It sounds like a Catch-22."

The third, and most effective way of dealing with your anger is to own it. *Confess it*—acknowledge your feelings! Take responsibility for them, and process them in an appropriate way. Vigorous physical exercise is often helpful in working off the energy generated by anger. And discussing the cause of your anger with a friend, or counselor, can help you process your feelings in a nondestructive way. Many people have found prayer to be a safe and effective way of expressing their angry thoughts and feelings. Once they tell God how they feel, and why they are angry, their anger is usually under control. An additional benefit is the insight they often receive while in prayer. Having completed this process, they are now ready to deal constructively with the conflict between themselves and their spouse.

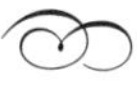

ACTION STEPS

- Ask yourself: "Is anger a problem for me? If so, in what way?"
- Ask yourself: "Is anger a problem for my spouse? If so, in what way?"
- Take some time with your spouse and discuss the role anger plays in your marriage. Is it constructive or destructive? How could it be better handled?

THOUGHTS FOR THE DAY

"We not only need to know how to deal with our anger in different ways at different times but also how most appropriately to match the right time with the right style of expression."[5]

—M. Scott Peck, M.D.

"I would say to all: Use your gentlest voice at home. . . ."

—Anonymous

SCRIPTURES FOR THE DAY

"He who guards his lips guards his life, but he who speaks rashly will come to ruin."

—PROVERBS 13:3

"A gentle answer turns away wrath, but a harsh word stirs up anger."

—PROVERBS 15:1

PRAYER

Lord, I have had to deal with anger my whole life, and many times I have failed. I have yielded to my anger, given vent to a torrent of hurtful words. As a result, I have wounded my spouse and children, driven peace from our home. Forgive me, Lord, for I have sinned Heal the wounds my reckless words have caused and set a watch over my lips. Let no angry word come from my mouth. In the name of Jesus I pray. Amen.

THE THINGS COUPLES FIGHT ABOUT

With a slight variation for the individual personalities, most couples quarrel about the same kinds of things. In extreme situations, there is conflict over the excessive use of drugs or alcohol, physical abuse and infidelity. In more moderate situations, couples argue about sex, money, in-laws, child rearing and affective needs.

As you might suspect, sex is a major source of conflict in many marriages, especially during the early years. In most cases, men normally get angry over the frequency, or perhaps I should say the infrequency, of sex. "I like sex two or three times a week," explains a young man. "My wife, however, would be very happy to be held and caressed and nothing more. She is a wonderful woman, and there is so much about our marriage that is good. But this is a problem for me."

Women, on the other hand, become angry when they feel used rather than loved. A harried wife and mother describes her feelings this way: "I love sex and have a need for it, but not when I am worn to a frazzle by my four kids, the car pool and housework. My need for affection is greater during times of stress, and my desire for sex is diminished. My husband thinks sex is affection. When I try to explain the difference, he does not understand." (This topic will be dealt with in greater depth in the section titled "Intimacy Is More Than Sex.")

Another common source of conflict is money. This point was driven home to me when I was just a boy and spending the summer with my aunt and uncle. One morning my uncle decided to buy a new ski boat. He invited my cousin and me to go with him when he went to pick it out. Well do I remember the excitement of choosing a sleek 16-foot outboard with a 75-horsepower Mercury engine. Once we had it outfitted with the required safety equipment, and two pairs of water skis, we pulled it home.

I followed my cousin into the house as he ran to tell his mother the good news. She didn't say anything, but a grim silence settled over the house. She was angry, there was no mistaking that, and for days we all went around as if we were walking on eggshells. None of us wanted to become the target of her brooding wrath. Later, we learned that she had wanted to carpet the living room, but was told, by my uncle, that they couldn't afford it. Given that information, it is not hard to understand her reaction when, a few days later, he showed up with a brand-new boat.

This scenario, or a similar one, is often the cause of marital conflict. When one of the partners makes a major purchase, like an appliance, or furniture or a new automobile, without consulting the other, the fur is sure to fly.

Another common argument revolves around control and accountability. When one partner, usually the husband, controls the purse strings and the other partner, usually the wife, is required to give an account of every penny spent, conflict is inevitable.

One couple, who had quarreled for years over this very issue, came up with an ingenious solution. Together they adopted a mutually acceptable budget that included an allowance for each of them. Responsibilities were divided between them. He would pay the bills and reconcile the checkbook. She would be responsible for buying groceries and managing the house. Since specific sums were allotted for given categories, she no longer had to ask his permission to buy groceries or the things she needed to run the house. An added benefit was the allowance. It could be spent any way they wanted and did not have to be accounted for.

Then there is the problem of in-laws. This conflict comes in as many forms as there are families. At the core, though, the issue is the same—allegiance. When the Bible says, "For this reason a man will leave his father and mother and be united to his wife, and they will become one flesh,"[1] it is talking about a transfer of allegiance. Before a man and woman can truly unite with one another and establish a family of their own, they each must leave their parental family; not just physically, but emotionally as well. They must each transfer their primary allegiance to the other.

One of the biggest adjustments in our marriage occurred right here. Alone, in our own home, there was no problem, but let us be with Brenda's parents, and the dynamics of our family relationships changed. This continued for several years, producing no little tension between us, before we could identify what was happening.

I love the Wallaces, and it was always a pleasure to be with them, but I often found myself struggling with resentment, especially toward Hildegard. Finally, I begin to pray about my feelings, and through prayer I was able to identify their source. The problem wasn't my mother-in-law, it was Brenda and me. When we were with her parents, the balance of allegiance shifted ever so subtly. Normally, Brenda was my wife first, Leah's mother second and then Hildegard's daughter. When we were with the Wallaces, the roles were exactly reversed she was Hildegard's daughter first, Leah's mother second and lastly she was my wife.

Once I identified the source of my frustration, we were able to talk about it and come to an understanding. Since we saw our parents so infrequently, it was natural for Brenda to give priority attention to her mother. I needed to understand this, accept it and stop resenting it. Brenda, on the other hand, determined to make a special effort to nurture our relationship, even when we were with her parents. It wasn't that I required more of her time, but just an awareness, on her part, that even "now," even "here," her first allegiance belonged to our marriage, rather than to her parental family.

As a result of our personal experience, we were able to counsel our daughter on the eve of her wedding. We told her: "After tomorrow you will be our daughter still, but not in the same way, not ever again. From that moment forward, your first allegiance, your first loyalty, belongs to your husband. Our home will no longer be your home. With your husband you will now make a new home of your own."

This does not mean that newlyweds are no longer in relationship with their parents, but only that the relationship has changed. Whereas before, it was "the" primary relationship in each of their lives, it has now become a secondary one. Still important, to be sure, but not as important.

Other areas of marital conflict include child rearing and affective needs, both of which will be dealt with in later sections of this book. Let it suffice to say that many of the conflicts couples experience are a direct result of their expectations of marriage. According to Dr. Joyce Brothers, "People want more from marriage and from love than older generations ever demanded or expected."[2] As a result they experience more conflict when their expectations are not met.

ACTION STEPS

- Both you and your spouse should prepare a list of the things that generate the most conflict in your marriage. Now compare your lists and discuss why you experience conflicts in these areas.
- Together discuss strategies for resolving these conflicts. See if you can each come up with two or three possible solutions for each issue.

THOUGHTS FOR THE DAY

"This is the first time in the history of the world that people have asked for intimacy, communication, sensuality and quality sex in their marriages."[3]

—Dr. Jessie Potter

"Unfulfilled expectations generate frustration with anger. The higher our expectations, and the more numerous our needs, the more often will we find ourselves blocked ... People differ greatly in the amount of frustration they can tolerate, but all of us have a flashpoint at which we experience a surge of anger. In marriage ... this can easily happen, because we find ourselves in a situation in which expectations are high, and frustration can often occur."[4]

—David and Vera Mace

SCRIPTURE FOR THE DAY

"Do not let any unwholesome talk come out of your mouths, but only what is helpful for building others up according to their needs, that it may benefit those who listen. And do not grieve the Holy Spirit of God, with whom you were sealed for the day of redemption. Get rid of all bitterness, rage and anger, brawling and slander, along with every form of malice. Be kind and compassionate to one another, forgiving each other, just as in Christ God forgave you."

—EPHESIANS 4:29-32

PRAYER

Lord, I thank You for those times in the past when You have given me insight into the source of my anger and frustration. And I thank You for giving me wisdom to deal with them constructively—Once again I come before You seeking help. Grant me both understanding and compassion that I may respond in love and not anger. In the name of Jesus I pray. Amen.

WARRIOR OR PROBLEM-SOLVER?

They sat on the couch in my office, glaring at each other. For nearly ten minutes they had argued vehemently, and now they sat in silence, having exhausted themselves without solving anything. Finally, I directed them to sit on the couch, side by side, shoulder to shoulder, facing straight ahead. When they were in position, I placed an empty chair directly in front of them.

"Imagine," I said, "that the thing you are arguing about is sitting in that chair leering at you. It's your enemy. It's the thing that is robbing your marriage of its peace and companionship."

They were a little skeptical, I could see that, but I had their attention nonetheless, so I continued. "You are both acting like the only way to resolve this issue is to win the argument. Consequently, you are going at each other tooth and nail. Eventually, one of you will probably prevail, but your marriage will be the poorer for it. Anytime one of you loses, both of you lose. Remember, you are on the same team. The issue is your common enemy."

Getting up, I handed each of them a yellow legal pad and a pen. "I want you to take the next five minutes and focus on that chair. Get a real good look at your enemy. Then I want you to define the issue. Write it out. Be specific. You will never be able to resolve this conflict until you can both identify the problem."

Once they agreed on the issue, I directed each of them to come up with three or four possible solutions. Only after they had written their solutions on the yellow legal pads did I allow them to resume the "argument." Of course, by then, their anger was gone, and they were able to concentrate on finding a solution, rather than on hurting each other.

Obviously, this tactic works best when there is a third party involved, but that does not mean that you cannot utilize it at home. Practice by using it when you have a difficult decision to make. Since you are not angry, it will be easier for you to interrupt the discussion in order to write out several possible solutions. If you get in a habit of doing this, you may be able to resolve minor marital conflicts before they become infused with anger.

Of course, if one of you is an intractable warrior, this isn't going to work. A warrior has to win at any cost. He isn't interested in resolving the conflict unless he comes out the winner. The problem-solver, on the other hand, has no interest in winning or losing. He only wants to resolve the issue so the marriage can function as God intended.

ACTION STEPS

- Are you a warrior or a problem-solver? Ask your spouse how he/she sees you.
- If you are a warrior, are you willing to change? You may need to make yourself accountable to a spiritually mature friend, or even join a support group.
- Change of this magnitude is impossible without God's help. Make a commitment right now to seek God's help on a daily basis.

THOUGHT FOR THE DAY

"Effective conflict-resolution communication focuses on *issues* rather than attacking personalities. This is the chief characteristic of productive, as distinguished from futile, arguments. Furthermore, conflict resolution deals with *specific issues* on which decisions and compromise action can be worked out. It stays away from global accusations and from tackling the whole problem all at once (a sure way to fail). The 'issue' in unproductive arguments is often only an excuse for attack upon the other partner. The hidden purpose is to increase one's own sense of power by 'putting the other down.'"[1]

—Howard and Charlotte Clinebell

SCRIPTURE FOR THE DAY

"He [Christ] died for us so that, whether we are awake or asleep, we may live together with him. Therefore encourage one another and build each other up....

"...Live in peace with each other ... Make sure that nobody pays back wrong for wrong, but always try to be kind to each other and to everyone else.

"Be joyful always; pray continually; give thanks in all circumstances, for this is God's will for you in Christ Jesus."

—I THESSALONIANS 5:10,11,13,15-18

PRAYER

Lord, I think I am a warrior by nature. I want to win no matter who gets hurt. Only now am I beginning to see how destructive that is, how unchristlike. I don't want to be this way, but I seem powerless to change myself. Change me, I pray. Make me the kind of person I ought to be. Teach me, O Lord, how to be kind, how to live at peace, especially with my family. In the name of Jesus I pray. Amen.

FIGHT FAIRLY AND SAVE YOUR MARRIAGE[1]

Marital quarrels are inevitable, and every couple will disagree sooner or later, even committed Christians. While conflict is uncomfortable, it is not necessarily bad. In fact, a "fair" fight can actually contribute to the quality of your marriage. If you can learn to use your quarrels to resolve your differences, then anger can be constructive rather than destructive. With that thought in mind, let me give you five rules for fighting fairly.

Rule # 1: Use "I" messages rather than "you" messages. An "I" message focuses on the speaker rather than the person being spoken to. For example, "You make me so mad" is a "you" message, and it attacks the person being addressed. On the other hand, "I feel angry when you do that," is an "I" message, and it focuses on the speaker, making him responsible for his feelings. By using "I" messages, you give your spouse a chance to evaluate what you are saying without feeling the need to defend himself or herself

Rule # 2: Practice reflective listening. Reflective listening is demanding under the best of conditions, and it can seem almost impossible when you are in the heat of an argument. But if you can force yourself to listen carefully before you speak, you will discover that the rewards are well worth the effort.

In the heat of an argument we are almost always tempted to defend ourselves, or at least to explain ourselves. Reflective listening forces us to control that defensive instinct. Instead of defending yourself, you might say: "It sounds like you feel hurt and angry when I make a major decision without consulting you."

A statement like that does at least two things. First, it lets your spouse know that you hear what he/she is saying and that his/her thoughts and feelings are important. Second, it allows him/her to clarify and expand until you truly understand why he/she feels the way he/she does. Practice reflective listening consistently, and you will not only grow in your understanding of each other, but you will resolve some thorny issues as well.

Rule # 3: Stick to the issue! Many couples never resolve anything when they fight because they can't stick to the issue. Let me illustrate: Perhaps you thoughtlessly discard your clothes all over the house. How does that make your wife feel? Angry? Unappreciated? Hurt?

There's a number of ways she can handle that situation. She can withdraw and punish you with silence. She can attack you by telling you what an insensitive slob you are. She can nag you with sarcastic remarks, "Thanks for helping me keep the house picked up. I've only worked on it all day." Or she can use an "I" message. Something like, "I feel unappreciated when you leave your clothes all over the house, especially after I've spent all day cleaning."

If you are like a lot of husbands, you are probably more interested in winning the fight than in solving the problem. In that case, you will probably change the subject and mount an attack. "When you clean out your sewing room you can talk to me about my dirty socks, but until then I don't want to hear it."

With those words the battle lines are drawn and the war is on. Now it's a full-fledged argument, and not the kind that solves anything either. This destructive nonsense will likely continue until bedtime and then you will probably go to bed, back to back, with anger heavy between you.

The problem here is a common one—an inability or an unwillingness to stick to the issue.

The next time you find yourself caught in the same old argument, why don't you ask yourself. "How can I help my husband/wife solve this?"—or even, "How can he/she help me solve this?" Instead of attacking each other, why not join forces and attack the issue?

Rule # 4: Don't hit below the belt. If you have been married for any length of time, you know where your spouse is vulnerable, you know how to hurt him/her, and he/she knows how to hurt you. I'm thinking of a man whose first wife left him for another man. When he asked her to come back, she laughed and ridiculed him. When he demanded an explanation, she said, "You're a lousy lover. You've never once satisfied me." Needless to say, he was devastated.

A couple of years passed, and he remarried. During a tender moment he shared that painful secret with his new wife. Some months later in the heat of battle she used it against him. "It's not hard to see why your first wife took a lover," she said cruelly.

That's what I mean by hitting below the belt. She won the argument, but the marriage was sorely wounded.

Rule # 5: Don't go to bed mad. Unresolved anger can turn into bitterness almost overnight. That's why Paul said, ".... let not the sun go down upon your wrath."[2] Nothing is more important than ending the conflict and renewing the relationship before calling it a day.

When forgiveness is freely given, and fully received, a miracle takes place. Anger dies. Hurt and bitterness are replaced with love. Tenderness takes up residence where hostility once reigned. Communication is restored, and old hurts are replaced by bright hopes. Once again marriage is a safe place in a demanding world.

ACTION STEPS

- Memorize the five steps to productive conflict resolution:
    1) Don't attack. Use "I" messages rather than "you" messages.
    2) Practice reflective listening.
    3) Stick to the issue.
    4) Don't hit below the belt.
    5) Don't go to bed mad.
- Make a covenant with your spouse that you will always "fight fairly." Now seal that covenant by committing it to God in prayer.

THOUGHT FOR THE DAY

"There is an old story about a sheepherder in Wyoming who would observe the behavior of wild animals during the winter. Packs of wolves, for example, would sweep into the valley and attack the bands of wild horses. The horses would form a circle with their heads at the center of the circle and kick out at the wolves, driving them away. Then the sheepherder saw the wolves attack a band of wild jackasses. The animals also formed a circle, but they formed it with their heads out toward the wolves. When they began to kick, they ended up kicking one another.

"People have a choice between being as smart as a wild horse or as stupid as a wild jackass. They can kick the problem or they can kick one another."[3]

—H. Norman Wright

SCRIPTURE FOR THE DAY

"Husbands, in the same way be considerate as you live with your wives, and treat them with respect as the weaker partner and as heirs with you of the gracious gift of life, so that nothing will hinder your prayers.

"Finally, all of you, live in harmony with one another; be sympathetic, love as brothers, be compassionate and humble. Do not repay evil with evil or insult with insult, but with blessing, because to this you were called so that you may inherit a blessing."

—I PETER 3:7-9

PRAYER

Lord, as heirs together of the gracious gift of life we commit our covenant to You. We agree together to practice the five rules for fighting fairly. Recognizing our weakness, and propensity for hurting one another, we call upon You for divine assistance. Enable us to do what we cannot do alone. Empower us to resolve our marital conflicts in ways that are constructive rather than destructive. In the name of Jesus we pray. Amen.

FIVE

Intimacy Is More Than Sex

SECTION 5

INTIMACY IS MORE THAN SEX

"To know another's body and movements so intimately that each moves in harmony with the other as a waltz partner—this is marriage. To lie down together at the end of a day, to stretch however briefly against the loved one while the physical tensions flee before the soft glory of flesh pressed against flesh; to lie in the dark and share the usually unspoken thoughts, the apologies and compliments each has repressed, the secret dreams and the precious visions—this is marriage. To cap these with a prayer, a shared moment of togetherness in the great ecology of the universe, is to build self into self inextricably as the roots of two sturdy trees mesh the ground of their being. For such, sleep itself becomes a form of intercourse."[1]

—Dorothy Samuel

A THEOLOGY OF SEX

What you believe about sex, or more particularly, what you believe the Bible says about sex, will have a profound influence on the sexual dimensions of your marriage. If you believe, as did one wife who sought my pastoral counsel, that sex is inherently evil, then you will experience no little difficulty enjoying the physically intimate aspects of marriage. Your marriage bed will be a stern place, inhabited by shame and guilt. And sex will be something to be endured rather than enjoyed.

This same wife went on to confess that she feared that her rather timid husband was unnatural in his sexual desires.

"What," I asked her, "do you mean by 'unnatural'?"

It wasn't easy for her to talk about these things, and she squirmed nervously in her chair before replying. Finally, she spoke, in an embarrassed tone. "He wants to see me when I have nothing on." Just telling me made her blush, but once the words were out she rushed on. "He doesn't think there is anything wrong with a husband and wife seeing each other naked. Sometimes he even asks me to let him come into the bathroom when I am bathing."

"There's one other thing," she continued, "but I don't know how to tell you." She fell silent, studying her nails intently, while chewing nervously on her lower lip. When I had just about given up hope that she would ever speak again, she closed her eyes, took a deep breath and said, "He wants us to do it with the lights on—have sex, I mean—you know, make love. Sometimes he even wants to do it in the daytime."

Where, you may be wondering, did she get such a distorted view of sex? There are two primary sources: family and church. In a misdirected effort to counter the promiscuity that is rampant today, these authority figures sometimes give young people the wrong message. Instead of teaching that sex, within the bonds of holy matrimony, is a gift from God, to be received with thanksgiving and celebrated without shame, they focus only on the sinful aspects of illicit sex. As a result, their children enter marriage with an erroneous theology of sex.

Unlearning bad theology is never easy, but it can be done. Jesus said, "...you will know the truth, and the truth will set you free."[2] What, then, is the truth about sex in marriage?

Sex was God's idea, and He called it good! "...male and female he created them. God blessed them and said to them, 'Be fruitful and increase in number....' God saw all that he had made, and it was very good...."[3]

Sex, as we have already noted, is a gift from God to be received with thanksgiving and celebrated without shame. It is designed to express love, cultivate intimacy, provide pleasure and propagate the race. When God brought the woman to the man, they "...were both naked, and they felt no shame."[4]

The Scriptures teach that the marriage bed is "undefiled,"[5] which means that a husband and wife are free to discover the sexual expressions that are most pleasurable to each of them. Of course, anything that is physically or psychologically damaging to either partner is off-limits. Such acts are not expressions of love, but exploitation.

Having said that, let me hasten to add: "Nothing whatever, except the law of service, forbids anything you might do. Neither shame nor guilt restricts you. All the fruit of Eden is yours and before you."[6]

"...may you rejoice in the wife of your youth.... may her breasts satisfy you always, may you ever be captivated by her love."[7]

The Scriptures also teach that sexual intercourse is a marital duty: "The husband should fulfill his marital duty to his wife, and likewise the wife to her husband. The wife's body does not belong to her alone but also to her husband. In the same way, the husband's body does not belong to him alone but also to his wife. Do not deprive each other except by mutual consent and for a time, so that you may devote yourselves to prayer. Then come together again so that Satan will not tempt you because of your lack of self-control."[8]

I shared all of this information with the aforementioned wife. She listened intently, but was unable to conceal her skepticism, which shouldn't be surprising. A lifetime of erroneous teaching is not unlearned in a single afternoon. It takes time and hard work.

Before we concluded our session, I pointed out that there are usually three steps required of the person who wants to change a behavior: 1) mental assent—he must be willing to replace his faulty thinking with a new belief, 2) conscious choice—he must consciously choose a new course of action, and 3) deliberate action—he must now act and live in ways that are in keeping with his new beliefs.

The person who puts these steps into practice will discover that his feelings do not automatically change with his beliefs. The first few times this wife undressed in front of her husband, she felt terribly guilty. On more than one occasion she was tempted to revert to her former, more inhibited self. Her faulty reasoning went something like this: "If nakedness is not wrong, then why do I still feel guilty?" In counseling, I was able to help her understand that she was dealing with a false guilt, one that was a product of her faulty theology of sex. Repeatedly I told her, "You will not be able to think yourself into right feelings, but if you continue to do the right thing, your emotions will come into line." And they did.

ACTION STEPS

- Write a theology of sex based on your current beliefs. Now write a second theology of sex based on the Scriptures.
- Compare your theology of sex with your spouse's. Spend some time discussing them and how they affect your sexual relationship.

THOUGHT FOR THE DAY

"What is sexually right for us? The answer is learned only *in* the marriage, by actually practicing sex together with a constant and dear concern for the other's experience and an open expression of one's own. Doing is discovery. Trust allows you both to act before you know. The dependability of your partner allows you to reveal your own deep feelings as you go. A humble hearing allows you to receive your partner's feelings clearly, without threat or misinterpretation. You *make* your own loving.

"'What,' he asks in the darkness, 'do you want me to do for you?'

"And she answers shamelessly, 'I don't know. Try something, and I'll tell you what I think.'

"And so he does. And so does she. They try many things. They have more than a night for experimentation. They have as many years as God gives them life."[9]

—Walter Wangerin, Jr.

SCRIPTURE FOR THE DAY

There are three things that are too amazing for me,
four that I do not understand:
the way of an eagle in the sky,
the way of a snake on a rock,
the way of a ship on the high seas,
and the way of a man with a maiden."

—PROVERBS 30:18

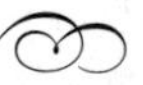

PRAYER

Lord, I thank You for godly parents who gave me a healthy and biblically sound theology of sex. I thank You for a spouse who is spontaneous and uninhibited in the expression of his/her love. Most of all I thank You for the gift of marriage and the joy of sex within this holy relationship. In Jesus' name I pray. Amen.

SEXUAL DIFFERENCES BETWEEN MEN AND WOMEN

If you have been married for any length of time, you have already discovered that you and your spouse are distinctly different sexual creatures. You may have even been tempted to wonder if there was something wrong with your husband/wife, or—God forbid—with yourself. Stop worrying. For reasons known only to God, men and women are created with different sexual needs and desires. As I'm sure you've already found out, these differences can be a source of confusion, and even conflict. If they cannot be discussed and accommodated, they will inevitably undermine your sexual intimacy and have a negative impact on your marriage.

Some of the more obvious differences find expression in the varied ways men and women respond to the sex act itself. A man can be quickly aroused to a climactic explosion, while a woman's sexual desires take time to build. Not infrequently he is finished before she is hardly started. And when the moment of his supreme pleasure is over, he will be overcome with sleep while she lies awake, staring at the ceiling. Let this happen a few times, and it is not difficult to understand why many young wives conclude that sex is vastly overrated.

It is a wise husband who teaches himself to be sensitive to his wife's needs and desires. With disciplined love he teaches his impatient body to wait until his wife has attained the same level of sexual arousal. Even then he does not demand a predetermined conclusion, but rather allows their love making to create its own ending. Although he must experience an orgasm in order to be satisfied, he has learned that there are times when his wife enjoys intercourse without the need for a climax. Even as he is sensitive to her need for complete fulfillment, he also honors her ability to experience pleasure without achieving an orgasm. He refuses to yield to the temptation to demand that she have an orgasm, or multiple orgasms, to prove his prowess as a lover.

Men and women also experience sexual stimulation in distinctly different ways. Sex, for a woman, is a small part of a total package. She is attracted to the man who makes her feel attractive and special, loved and secure. When the emotional climate in their marriage is calm, when he spends time with her, when they do things together and share deeply, she finds herself in the mood for intimacy. In other words, her mind—what she is thinking—and her emotions—what she is feeling—play a significant role in her sexual desire.

While a man's emotions may affect his sexual performance, it is usually to a much lesser degree and often doesn't manifest itself until midlife and beyond. In the early years of marriage, almost nothing dampens his desire. Not job pressures, physical fatigue or even marital quarrels, as many a young wife can attest. Virtually every wife has had more than a little experience with the disgruntled male who comes home from work in a foul mood, snaps at her every time she says anything during dinner and then retreats to the den where he spends the rest of the evening sulking in front of the television.

Having failed to dispel his grouchiness, she finally gives up and goes upstairs to prepare for bed. He arrives just in time to catch a glimpse of her as she slips into bed, and he's suddenly aroused. His interest is almost incomprehensible to her. Just minutes ago she couldn't get a civil word out of him, and now he's all "lovey-dovey." Of course, given her own sexual nature, it is more than a little difficult for her to generate a response. All of which just goes to show that while her sexual desires are strongly influenced by what she thinks and feels, his are distinctly physical. Let him get a glimpse of his nearly nude wife, and everything else is forgotten.

Women are usually more concerned about propriety. The time and place have to be appropriate. They need privacy. They fear being overheard or interrupted. Well do I remember the strain this placed on our relationship in the early years of our marriage. We lived more than a thousand miles from our parents, and every year our vacations were spent going "home." Although I enjoyed seeing our folks every bit as much as Brenda did, after a few days I grew frustrated. The problem? Brenda felt uncomfortable about making love in her parents' home. What if they heard us?

What if they knew what we were doing? Ultimately, Brenda was able to overcome her inhibitions, but for a time it was a real source of tension for us.

It is critical for both partners to recognize and accept their sexual differences. He is not some kind of sex maniac. She is not frigid. They are different, one from the other, and it is these very differences that challenge their love to grow. As he subjugates his desires so he can meet hers, his love grows. As she accommodates his needs, her love grows. No longer is their sexuality a selfish thing, thinking only of its own fulfillment. Now it has been sanctified by their love, and it has become a way of expressing their spiritual and emotional connectedness.

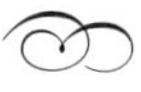

ACTION STEPS

- Not infrequently our sexual differences generate anger, causing us to do and say things that hurt our spouse. Take a few minutes and remember any of the hurtful things you may have done. Now apologize specifically for each one and seek your spouse's forgiveness.
- Briefly discuss ways in which you can be more sensitive to each other, in all areas, but especially in this area.

THOUGHT FOR THE DAY

"If I had the power to communicate only one message to every family in America, I would specify the importance of romantic love to every aspect of feminine existence. It provides the foundation for a woman's self-esteem, her joy in living, and her sexual responsiveness. Therefore, the vast number of men who are involved in bored, tired marriages—find themselves locked out of the bedroom—should know where the trouble possibly lies. Real love can melt an iceberg."[1]

—Dr. James Dobson

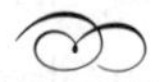

SCRIPTURE FOR THE DAY

"The Lord God said, 'It is not good for the man to be alone. I will make a helper suitable for him.'…

"…But for Adam no suitable helper was found. So the Lord God caused the man to fall into a deep sleep; and while he was sleeping, he took one of the man's ribs and closed up the place with flesh. Then the Lord God made a woman from the rib he had taken out of the man, and he brought her to the man.

"The man said, 'This is now bone of my bones and flesh of my flesh; she shall be called "woman," for she was taken out of man.'

"For this reason a man will leave his father and mother and be united to his wife, and they will become one flesh.

"The man and his wife were both naked, and they felt no shame."

—GENESIS 2:18,20-25

PRAYER

Lord, I have to confess that I have often resented the sexual differences between men and women. They cause so many conflicts. I've even been so presumptuous as to think that You had made a mistake or that You were just playing a cruel joke. Only now am I beginning to grasp something of Your wisdom. It's these differences that separate us from the animals. It's these differences that change our sexual desires from a self-serving thing to an act of love. Redeem my sexual desires, Lord. Make them a holy thing that I may use to love and serve my beloved. In the name of Jesus l pray. Amen.

WHAT DOES A BROKEN DISHWASHER HAVE TO DO WITH SEX?

As we have already noted, a woman's sexual desires are intertwined with her emotions. Hassles that most men would consider minor annoyances can totally distract her; can cause her to lose all interest in sex, at least for the time being. Initially, we focused on the effect that marital difficulties can have on her sexual desires. In this chapter we turn our attention to emotional detractions in general—problems with the children, an argument with a friend, even the stress resulting from a broken appliance.

Let me illustrate with a story of a couple we'll call Don and Karen. About midmorning Don begins feeling amorous so he calls Karen and invites her to lunch. Excitedly she accepts, and then spends the next twenty minutes trying to find someone to stay with the children. Once that's done, she turns her attention to herself. After a quick shower, she carefully applies makeup and does her hair, all the while thinking about Don. It's been so long since he's done anything like this. She wants to look her best, wants everything to be perfect.

Glancing at her watch, she realizes that she's late. Rushing out the door, she calls instructions over her shoulder to the baby-sitter. After a hurried drive downtown, she turns into the restaurant parking lot just as Don is getting out of his car. *Perfect,* she thinks, giving him her warmest smile.

Although they only have an hour, they make the most of it. And by the time lunch is over, they are both in a romantic mood. Before going their separate ways, they make plans to devote the entire evening to love. She will feed the children early and get them ready for bed. He will rent a video they have both been wanting to see.

He returns to the office in a better mood than he's known in days. His secretary catches him humming the musical theme from "Somewhere in Time." With a knowing smile she comments, "That must have been some lunch."

Alone again, he thinks, "We should do this more often." He makes a mental note to have his secretary put it on his calendar. If a client hadn't canceled lunch today, he would not have had time for Karen. *Thank God,* he thinks, *for small favors, and for a wife who is willing to be spontaneous.*

When Karen arrives home, she finds herself confronted by a domestic crisis. The dishwasher has gone on the blink, and the repairman can't come until the day after tomorrow. To make matters worse, the baby-sitter has dirtied every dish in the kitchen. The baby is cranky all afternoon, making it impossible for her to clean up the mess in the kitchen. By five o'clock he is running a fever of 101 degrees, and she is at her wit's end. Whatever romantic feelings she had at lunch have long since fled.

About six o'clock Don walks in with that "come hither" look in his eye only to discover, not the bewitching wife he expected, but an exhausted mother. Being the sensitive man that he is, he spends the evening helping Karen with the children. Surely, he reasons, once they are in bed we can make up for lost time.

Once again he is in for a surprise. Romance is the furthest thing from Karen's mind. Collapsing on the couch, after the little ones are finally tucked in, she regales him with a blow-by-blow account of her dreadful afternoon. He listens with thinly disguised impatience. By now he's ready to promise her anything—a new set of china, the latest super-deluxe dishwasher, a vacation to Hawaii, anything, but to no avail. She refuses to recapture her early romantic mood.

Depending on how determined he is, they may still make love, but I can assure you it won't be anything like they had planned.

What happened? That's what most husbands who find themselves in that kind of situation would like to know. What, they wonder, does a broken dishwasher have to do with making love? And most wives, in that situation, end up wondering why they ever married such an insensitive clod.

In truth, she is not overreacting, and he is not an insensitive clod. What we have here is just another demonstration of the sexual differences between men and women. Let me say it again: Hassles that most men would consider minor annoyances can cause her to lose all interest in sex, at least for the time being. And if a couple doesn't understand what's happening, things can rapidly go from bad to worse.

ACTION STEPS

- Recall the last time something like this happened to you. How did you handle it? What will you do differently if it should happen again?
- **For him:** Read, or reread, *What Wives Wish Their Husbands Knew About Women* by Dr. James Dobson.[1]
- **For her:** Read, or reread, *Understanding the Man in Your Life* by H. Norman Wright.[2]
- Share the insights you discover with each other. Let this material serve as a springboard for discussion.

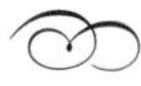

THOUGHTS FOR THE DAY

One woman describes her husband's feelings about sex:

"When he's upset or mad or insecure, he wants sex. I guess it reassures him. But I wish he would talk about the feelings. When I get home from work and I'm wound up with a lot of baggage, I want to talk about it. When he comes home that way, he doesn't want to talk, he wants sex. When I'm sad, what I need is a shoulder to cry on and someone to hear me out. When he's sad, he wants to be seduced out of his feelings."[3]

—Michael McGill

"A physician named Schwab described the difficulties a woman may experience in playing the three unique roles expected of her; she must be a wife, mistress, and mother. A loving wife who is diligently maintaining her home and caring for the needs of her family is unlikely to feel like a seductive mistress who tempts her husband into the bedroom. Likewise, the requirements of motherhood are at times incompatible with the alternate roles of wife and mistress. Though these 'assignments' seem contradictory, a woman is often asked to switch from one to another on short notice. Her husband can help by getting her away from the wife and mother responsibilities when it is time for her to be his mistress."[4]

—Dr. James Dobson

SCRIPTURE FOR THE DAY

"On the seventh day the child died....

"Then David got up from the ground. After he had washed, put on lotions and changed his clothes, he went into the house of the Lord and worshiped. Then he went to his own house, and at his request they served him food, and he ate ...

"Then David comforted his wife Bathsheba, and he went to her and lay with her. She gave birth to a son, and they named him Solomon...."

—2 SAMUEL 12:18,20,24

PRAYER

For him:

Lord, I can identify with the husband who found comfort and encouragement when he made love with his wife. Help me to accept my feelings without projecting them on my wife. When she is hurting, let me remember that sex is probably not what she needs. Help me to hold her and listen without offering advice. Let my love be a covering that warms her against the chill of grief.

For her:

Lord, I can identify with the wife who found comfort in being held and listened to. But help me to remember that I must be a wife and a mistress to my husband as well as a mother to our children. Make me more attentive to his feelings and frustrations. Help me to learn to comfort and assure him in the way he needs it most, through expressions of physical love.

In the name of Jesus I pray. Amen.

CHARLIE SHEDD'S FOLLY

When I was just nineteen years old, and in my first year of Bible college, I was privileged to hear Charlie Shedd speak in chapel. He was not only a successful pastor, but a best-selling author as well, having written several books, including *Letters to Karen,*[1] and *Letters to Philip.*[2] I was planning to be married in a few weeks, and since he was best known for his books on marriage, I hung on his every word.

About money, he said, "Give 10 percent, save 10 percent, and spend the rest with thanksgiving." About the family, he said, "Wherever Dad sits is the head of the table." There's more, but the thing I remember best is what he said about keeping the home fires burning. With a twinkle in his eye, he told all of us young preachers in the making, "No matter how financially strapped you may be, always buy your wife a beautiful negligee at least once a year."

Well, shortly thereafter, Brenda and I were married, and I became the pastor of a small rural church in Colorado. It was a challenging situation. Sunday morning attendance averaged less than thirty people, counting the children. And we were, in Charlie Shedd's words, strapped! Our total income that first year was barely twenty-six hundred dollars. Still, I managed to buy Brenda a beautiful nightgown that year, and each of the following three years.

Imagine my surprise when she became tearfully angry upon receiving her fourth nightgown in as many years. Refusing it, she said, "All you ever buy me are negligees. And it's not even for me, not really."

"What do you mean, it's not for you?" I demanded, more confused than angry.

"It's for you," she said. "I'm supposed to put it on and look sexy—for you, for your pleasure. Then we'll make love, and I'll feel used. Just once I wish you would buy me a new dress."

Well, to say the least, I was hurt and angry. If I could have gotten my hands on Charlie Shedd, I would have strangled him. Still, after I had time to work through my feelings, I began to understand what Brenda was saying.

The issue wasn't just a new dress, though that would have been nice. What Brenda wanted, and needed, was a public demonstration of my love—something that said to the world, "I love this woman. I'm glad she's my wife."

Now, a new dress is not the only way to do that, and not necessarily the best way. Belatedly, I discovered that small gestures of affection, like holding her hand in public, or taking her arm as we crossed the street, made her feel special, as did a timely compliment. And you can be assured that feeling special is an important part of intimacy, especially to a woman.

As a young husband, I found the mystery of the female mind to be unfathomable at times, and I still do. A rule of thumb, which has proved helpful, however, is to remember that we husbands must express our love in ways that make our wives feel loved, rather than in ways that make us feel loving. That too, is an important part of intimacy, for both men and women.

ACTION STEPS

- Ask your spouse what you do that makes him/her feel loved. At a marriage retreat, one lady said she felt very loved when her husband warmed her side of the bed before she got into it at night. I feel especially loved when Brenda brews a cup of espresso for me without being asked.
- Take special note of the things your spouse mentions and make it a point to do at least one of them every day.

THOUGHT FOR THE DAY

"During the first years of our own marriage my wife, Linda, would occasionally tell me how much it meant to her for me to continue to observe some of the etiquette of courting. For instance, if we were getting into the car, she wanted me to take the trouble to go over to her side of the car and open the door for her. If you had asked me if I knew that was important to her, I would have answered, 'Yes.' If you had asked me how high on her list of ways of expressing love it was, I would have said, 'Oh, about number 32.'

"That's because it was about that low on my own list. If you would have told me that opening the car door for her was *third* on my wife's list of priorities, I would have told you to get lost. After all, I knew my wife better than you. But it was third on her list!

"I was blown away when I first learned that. It meant that if I wanted to express my love and care in a way that was important to her, a simple act like opening the car door would do it."[3]

—Rich Buhler

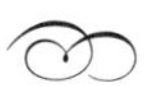

SCRIPTURE FOR THE DAY

"This is how we know what love is: Jesus Christ laid down his life for us. And we ought to lay down our lives for our brothers. If anyone has material possessions and sees his brother in need but has no pity on him, how can the love of God be in him? Dear children, let us not love with words or tongue but with actions and in truth."

—I JOHN 3:16-18

PRAYER

Lord, remind me how often I have been loved by family and friends, and especially by my spouse. Sometimes I forget. How undeserving I am of their love, but how needful. Without it, I would be an orphan in this world, a man/woman without a place to belong, having no family or home. Open my heart to those I love, especially my life's companion, so I can give them the love they so hunger for. In the name of Jesus I pray. Amen.

INTIMACY IS MORE THAN SEX

Some years ago Ann Landers wrote an article for *Family Circle* titled "What 100,000 Women Told Ann Landers." In it she shared the results of a survey in which she asked her women readers: "Would you be content to be held close and treated tenderly and forget about 'the act'?" Seventy-two percent of the respondents said yes, they would be content just to be held close and treated tenderly and forget about the sex act. Interestingly enough, 40 percent of those who said yes were under forty years of age.

Ann concluded: "...a great many women choose affection over sex. Those yes votes were saying, 'I want to be valued. I want to feel cared about. Tender words and loving embraces are more rewarding than an orgasm produced by a silent, mechanical, self-involved male.'"[1]

If you are a man, you may feel misunderstood, or even threatened by that, but I hope not. My purpose for including it here is not to imply that men are insensitive creatures interested only in their own sexual fulfillment. My experience as a man, and as a minister who has counseled with hundreds of men, tells me that simply is not the case. Granted, many husbands may appear to be one-dimensional in their marital relationship, but that is only because they have not learned to express their deepest feelings in nonsexual ways.

For the man, sex is a whole lot more than a physical act. It is his way of expressing his need for closeness, tenderness and deep sharing. It is his heart's cry for intimacy. In truth, he experiences a haunting sadness when his wife contributes nothing more than her body. He may not be able to explain his need to her, but I can assure you, he hungers for emotional closeness as much as she does.

The real problem here is not sex, but communication. Both men and women make the mistake of assuming that their partner feels and responds the same way as they do to the relational and emotional factors in their lives. This simply is not the case. When a woman feels lonely or depressed, the last thing she wants is sex. She wants her husband to hold her while she pours out the pain in her heart. She longs to be understood, to be comforted with nonsexual acts of affection, like a hug or a shared cup of tea. This, for her, is intimacy.

When a man feels alone, or misunderstood, he doesn't want to talk about it. Indeed, he can't talk about it, for he has no words to express the pain he feels. Instead, he wants to make love with his wife. He wants to resolve his loneliness the only way he knows how—sexually. What he cannot express in words, he communicates in the force of his loving. This, for him, is intimacy.

In truth, true marital intimacy occurs on both the emotional and the physical level. It involves both talking and touching, both nonsexual and sexual acts of tenderness and affection. In *The Intimate Marriage,* Howard and Charlotte Clinebell write: "Sexual intimacy is rooted in a biological drive pushing toward the discharge of sexual tension. This is the physiological basis of sexual attraction in all animals. But in man [humans] there develops a unique blend of the physiological and the psychological. The physical need for release of sexual tension is intertwined with a variety of psychological needs: for the security and warmth of body-closeness and stroking; for feeling loved, nurtured, cared about; for affirmation of one's masculinity or femininity .... Deep soul—and body—satisfying sex is never simply physical."[2]

They go on to say, "A marriage is vital to the extent that there is a uniting of these two forms of intimacy—physical and psychological.... The wedding ceremony contains an implicit truth about relationships in the phrase, 'love, honor and cherish.' A man and woman cannot really love deeply [become truly intimate] unless they also honor (esteem, appreciate, respect) and cherish (nurture, prize, hold dear) each other. The total quality and value of the relationship affects the meaning and satisfaction derived from sexual intercourse."[3]

With these insights the Clinebells have identified both the initial and the ultimate purpose of marriage—intimacy, oneness. The Scriptures declare, "For this reason a man will leave his father and mother and be united to his wife, *and they will become one flesh*"[4] (Italics mine).

Before Eve, Adam was alone, and it was not good. Although he shared a special relationship with all of God's creation, he was still alone in the deepest part of his soul. Even though he walked with God in the garden, and communed with Him as friend with friend, there remained a part of him that was achingly alone. The Scriptures declare: "...But for Adam no suitable helper was found."[5]

Where could he find his soul mate, that one who would finally end his aloneness? Not in the animal kingdom, for there was none like him. Nor in relationship with God, for that is intimacy on an altogether different plane. Only in marriage could he find the intimacy to satisfy his heart's hunger to know and be known. Only in marriage could he find the intimacy to satisfy his need for closeness and caring. Only in marriage could he find "flesh of his flesh and bone of his bone," to satisfy his need for sexual fulfillment.

So "...the Lord God made a woman from the rib he had taken out of the man, and he brought her to the man ... The man and his wife were both naked, and they felt no shame."[6]

They were intimate; they had no secrets to hide from each other. They were fully known, each to the other, and they were not ashamed. They had a transparent relationship built on love and trust.

Sexually, they were naked and not ashamed. Because they knew each other, in a way that only a husband and wife can know one another, they were joyously uninhibited in their sexuality. They were made for each other, that's what God said, so they took joy in their physical love.

Because they were one, because they were truly bonded emotionally, they could give themselves to each other sexually without reservation. And because of their joyous and uninhibited physical union, their emotional intimacy was complete. Without their blessed oneness, the physical act of making love would have been just that—a physical act—empty and unfulfilling; the merging of their flesh without the touching of their souls. That's loneliness of the most haunting kind. Yet, without the expression of their physical love, their emotional and spiritual intimacy would have been incomplete.

Marriage, as God meant it to be, brings it all together—the bread of love to nourish the spirit, the cup of forgiveness to wash our wounds and forgive our failures, to restore our blessed oneness. Nakedness that nothing need be hidden, transparency that we may at last know ourselves because finally we are known, and physical love that our aloneness might be swallowed up in the body of our beloved, that our love might give birth to a family.

In reality, what 100,000 women told Ann Landers is exactly what the Bible has been teaching for millenniums: Sex without intimacy is empty and unfulfilling. The need those women expressed for closeness and touching is simply an ageless echo of Adam's hunger to belong, to be truly united with that one who was a part of him, his other self, even as he was her other self. These needs can find their fulfillment only in marriage, but not in just any kind of marriage. It must be marriage as God intended. A marriage in which two individuals are committed to one another for life. A marriage in which there is mutual respect, deep sharing, kindness, affection and genuine love, as well as sexual intimacy.

ACTION STEPS

In *Why Men Don't Get Enough Sex and Women Don't Get Enough Love* authors Diane Dunaway and Jonathan Kramer have developed ten steps to help couples improve their communication and their intimacy. Let me suggest that you implement them in your own marriage.

For the woman:

1) Let him know when you need help with chores or kids; reinforce him by thanking him.

2) Make him feel special and loved, even if he appears confident.

3) Learn how he expresses himself (Male-speak).

4) Develop the traits of the six Inner Women he seeks—lover, cheerleader, mother, best friend, animal tamer and competent adult.

5) Teach him to be aware of his feelings; try to understand the male perspective of love.

6) Add romance to your lives instead of always waiting for him to do something; set the mood for intimacy.

7) Give affection openly, assertively and frequently, teaching him how to become more intimate.

8) Encourage him as he tries to discover your natural sexuality.

For the man:

1) Help her around the house to show you care.

2) Help her feel good about herself, telling her daily what you love about her.

3) Learn her way of expressing herself (Fem-speak).

4) Develop the traits of the four Inner Men she looks for—hero, playmate, friend, lover.

5) Get more in touch with your feelings; be more accepting of her.

6) Become more romantic through small daily gestures and occasional spontaneous outings.

7) Learn more subtle cues to turn her on and initiate lovemaking.

8) Concentrate on foreplay; remember, a woman needs to feel good before sex.

For both:

1) Plan and initiate fun activities.

2) Connect sex with love.

THOUGHT FOR THE DAY

"You never made
A lamp base out of a Cracker Jack box,
An extra room out of an unused closet,
Or a garden out of a pile of clay.
All you ever made was
A woman out of me."[7]

—Lois Wyse

SCRIPTURE FOR THE DAY

"Now Isaac had come from Beer Lahai Roi, for he was living in the Negev. He went out to the field one evening to meditate, and as he looked up, he saw camels approaching. Rebekah also looked up and saw Isaac. She got down from her camel and asked the servant, 'Who is that man in the field coming to meet us?'

"'He is my master,' the servant answered. So she took her veil and covered herself.

"Then the servant told Isaac all he had done. Isaac brought her into the tent of his mother Sarah, and he married Rebekah. So she became his wife, and he loved her; and Isaac was comforted after his mother's death."

—GENESIS 24:62-67

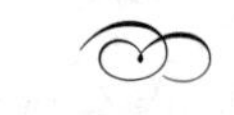

PRAYER

Lord, I thank You for the gift of marriage. There is nothing in all the world dearer than the intimacy I have found with my beloved. Within the circle of his/her love I have found the wholeness for which my heart hungered. Even in the hard times, when the feelings of love seemed to have disappeared, the commitment of marriage sustained us, kept us together, until the feelings returned. Continue to work with us. Make our marriage all You intended marriage to be. In the name of Jesus I pray. Amen.

SIX

Keeping Romance in Marriage

"Do the unexpected! Claudia will never forget the day Dave came in with three red roses and said, 'Pack your bag. We're leaving in thirty minutes!' Remember, Dave is the romantic!

"Off we went to a wonderful little hotel in the Vienna woods about thirty minutes from where we lived. Claudia wondered why they looked at her so curiously when we checked in. Dave had previously chosen the hotel and told them he had a very special lady friend he wanted to bring for a getaway. To this day, Claudia is convinced that the staff didn't think we were married. Dave's reaction? 'If you're going to have a romantic affair, have it with your mate!' And that's just what we did."[1]

—Dave and Claudia Arp

KEEPING ROMANCE IN YOUR MARRIAGE

Dr. James Dobson says, "Love can perish when a husband works seven days a week, when there is no time for romantic activity, when he and his wife forget how to talk to each other."

He concludes "...that 90 percent of the divorces that occur each year involve an extremely busy husband who is in love with his work and who tends to be somewhat insensitive, unromantic, and noncommunicative, married to a lonely, vulnerable, romantic woman who has severe doubts about her worth as a human being." He then adds, with a touch of gallows humor, "They become a matched team: He works like a horse and she nags."[2]

I think that pretty well describes the average marriage and, sad to say, it is not a very flattering picture. Each of us could probably add our own personal flavor, a specific incident or two, but the overall picture would still be the same. Far too many of us have allowed the stress of living to crowd romance right out of our marriage. And we're the losers. Gone from marriage, or at least significantly diminished, are tenderness and intimacy, not to mention joy.

Does that description fit your marriage, perhaps, painfully so? Thinking about it now, you may even be tempted with anger or, worse yet, despair. How you deal with your pain is critically important for it will determine the climate of your marriage and the shape of your relationship. Some couples simply make peace with their pain; they give up their dreams and live out their lives in mediocrity. They are together, but not intimate. Silence becomes a way of life for them.

While this unfulfilling mediocrity is better than outright hostility, it falls far short of the marital relationship God intends. In truth, marriage is both a gift and a discipline. God gives us each other and the tools for cultivating our marital intimacy, but it is up to us to work the soil of our relationship all the days of our lives. Only then will we know the true meaning of holy matrimony.

In marriage, little things mean a lot, especially to a woman. In fact, they can make the difference between a mediocre marriage and a really good one, one in which romance is alive and well. It's usually not the expensive gifts or the foreign vacations that determine the quality of a marital relationship, but the little things. A love note or an "unbirthday" card for her. A kind word, help with the children, a listening ear, the feeling that we really care. This is the stuff of which marital romance is made!

ACTION STEPS

- Recall the last time you shared a romantic moment with your spouse. Where were you? What were you doing? How long ago was it?
- Ask your spouse to remember his/her favorite romantic moment. Ask him/her to explain what made it so special.
- Romantic moments seldom just happen, they have to be carefully planned by at least one spouse. With that in mind, begin making plans right now for your next romantic interlude.

THOUGHT FOR THE DAY

"That year of our resurrection Thanne and I spent three days alone at a cabin in Kentucky. It had a tin roof, and the rains came down. In my memory, love sounds like the ceaseless drumming of autumn rains on a metal roof, both light and loud, so loud sometimes we couldn't hear each other; we could only be. And it smells clean. And love has an October bite—the same sharp chill that bit us on county roads in rural Illinois so long ago."[3]

—Walter Wangerin, Jr.

SCRIPTURE FOR THE DAY

"My lover spoke and said to me, 'Arise, my darling, my beautiful one, and come with me.

See! The winter is past; the rains are over and gone.

Flowers appear on the earth; the season of singing has come, the cooing of doves is heard in our land.

The fig tree forms its early fruit; the blossoming vines spread their fragrance.

Arise, come, my darling; my beautiful one, come with me.'"

—SONG OF SONGS 2:10-13

PRAYER

Lord, forgive me for taking my beloved for granted. Forgive me for allowing the demands of living—job pressures, parenting, financial concerns—to crowd romance out of our marriage. Give me another chance, and with Your help I will do better this time. In the name of Jesus I pray. Amen.

CHERISH THE MEMORIES OF YESTERDAY

Brenda and I have been married for nearly forty-two years, and during that time we have developed some principles that help us keep romance in our marriage. We have learned to cherish the memories of yesterday, to savor the joys of today and to nurture the promise of tomorrow.

Some of our memories are tenderly poignant, like the birth of our daughter Leah. Others are hysterically funny, at least in retrospect. Like the first time we had guests for dinner at the parsonage in Holly, Colorado. Right after we said grace, we heard a splashing noise in the kitchen, and discovered a mother mouse and her five babies swimming in the soapy dishwater. Thankfully, our guests were "country folk" and unfazed by it all.

Then there's the memory of the moths—Miller bugs is what we called them. They invaded us every summer, turning our house into an insect farm. I was disgusted, but Brenda made the best of a difficult situation by turning it into a game. After switching off all the lights, she turned on the gas burners on the kitchen range, and fried those dive-bombing bugs!

Not once did she complain; there were no tearful depressions, not even envy toward those pastors who were faring better than we. As you've probably already concluded, Brenda has an amazing ability to be content in all situations. Thinking about it now, these many years later, I realize again how fortunate I was. How fortunate I am.

Some of our memories just happened. I mean, there is no way we could have planned for either the mice or the moths, nor would we want to. More often than not, though, our memorable moments came about as the result of careful planning and considerable forethought. That's not to say you can plan a memory, but you can and must prepare for it.

For instance, to celebrate the completion of *The Rhythm of Life*[1] (one of my early books), we went to dinner with our daughter and her boyfriend. The two of them, with Brenda's help, planned the entire evening. They bought a cardboard top hat and filled it with slips of paper, upon which they had written questions relating to me. Things like: "What's your favorite memory of Richard?" or "What's the most embarrassing thing Richard ever did?" or "Out of all the things Richard has written, what is your favorite?" Of course, each time one of them answered a question I had to wear that fake top hat, to the delight of those who were dining nearby. Needless to say, that evening ranks right up there near the top on my hit parade of memories.

One of Brenda's favorite memories is of the week we spent together, in a rustic cabin, high in the Rockies, immediately following Leah's wedding. During the day we picnicked and rode horseback. At night we read books by kerosene lamplight, reminisced about Leah's childhood, wondering again how it could have slipped away so quickly.

Then there is Emerald Point. As a silver anniversary gift to ourselves, Brenda and I purchased 3.5 acres on Beaver Lake in Northwest Arkansas. We christened it Emerald Point because it is situated on a point of land that juts out into the most brilliant emerald green water I have ever seen. Immediately, we began planning and dreaming of building a small cabin where we could get away: a place where I could write without distractions, and where our grandchildren could spend time with us.

After nearly two years we were finally ready to begin construction. With an air of excitement we drove onto our property in late March and set up camp. Our friends could hardly believe what we were doing. They simply could not imagine elegant Brenda living in a tent, for weeks, while we built our cabin.

As luck would have it, we had one of the coldest and wettest springs in history. Night after night, the temperatures hovered around freezing, while an incessant downpour turned our tent into a soggy shelter. Once again Brenda saved a miserable situation with her comic relief.

It's not that she tries to be funny, she just is. Take, for instance, her improvised sleepwear. Every night, with deliberate extravagance, she donned two pairs of thermal underwear, wool socks and a fur hat that covered her entire head and tied under her chin. The finished product looked hilarious, sending us both into spasms of laughter. After making an outrageous display of modeling her "lingerie" in the damp confines of our frigid tent, she finally joined me under a heaping mound of quilts. When she whispered good-night, just before blowing out the lantern, I could see her breath. It was that cold! But we were warm beneath the blanket of laughter that echoed softly in the dark.

Now that our cabin is finished, we look back and wonder how we did it. I don't think we would try it again, but we wouldn't trade anything for the memories either.

When the tough times come, and believe me they will, you look back at all you've been through together, both the good times and the bad, and you say, "We can make it!" When you are tempted to give up, to wonder if life might not be better if you each went your separate way, you remember all you've shared and you realize that you have too much invested in this relationship to give up now. That's the power of shared memories.

ACTION STEPS

- Recall two or three special memories of you and your spouse. Replay them in your mind, savoring again their special joy, their poignancy.
- Plan a special time and place to share those memories with your spouse.
- Agree together to make memory-making and sharing a high priority in your marriage.

THOUGHT FOR THE DAY

"I remember you, Thanne, in flashes, in frozen images all throughout these eighteen years. It's as though I have snapshots of you on the wall beside me. The times are fixed by the love that shone in them, caught them, and kept them in my memory.

"You are standing in the huge garden we raised in the country, your face turned toward me. You're wearing shorts and a halter and a granny apron. The apron is caught up by the corners in each of your hands, and you are leaning slightly backward because the apron is lumpy-full of a load of tomatoes. It is a summer's abundance. You are smiling at me, calling, I think, some casual word. I don't remember the word. Rather, I remember this, that your thin body, so willingly bearing so swollen a load, pierced me with a sudden, nearly painful love. I thought, *I was the one who desired the garden. But you are the one who picks tomatoes, and you know how to preserve them...*

"The more I look at these memories, the more I realize that their radiance is unearthly, though you are no more than an earthly woman. It's a nimbus, Thanne, a divinity. It's a sort of cloud of glory that shines around my remembering and our marriage."[2]

—Walter Wangerin, Jr.

SCRIPTURE FOR THE DAY

"All night long on my bed I looked for the one my heart loves; I looked for him but did not find him.

I will get up now and go about the city, through its streets and squares; I will search for the one my heart loves.

So I looked for him but did not find him.

The watchmen found me as they made their rounds in the city.

'Have you seen the one my heart loves?'

Scarcely had I passed them when I found the one my heart loves.

I held him and would not let him go till I had brought him to my mother's house, to the room of the one who conceived me."

—SONG OF SONGS 3:1-4

PRAYER

Lord, my memories are a mixed bag. Some of them are so painful I cannot bear the thought of them. Some are so precious I can hardly bear to speak of them. How can this be? How can two people create such a hodgepodge of remembrances? Give me now, I pray, the gift of selective memory. Let me forget the painful mistakes of the past without ever forgetting the lessons learned. Let me now embrace the joys of our shared past. May these memories become a vision shaping our future together. In the name of Jesus I pray. Amen.

SAVOR THE JOYS OF TODAY

"One of the most tragic things I know about human nature," said Dale Carnegie, "is that all of us tend to put off living. We are all dreaming of some magical rose garden over the horizon, instead of enjoying the roses that are blooming outside our windows today."[1]

Young couples are especially susceptible to this temptation. It is so easy to say, "Wait until we've saved enough money for a down payment on the house we want, and then we'll take a vacation." Then it's, "Once we get the house furnished, we'll take that trip we've been planning." Or worse yet, they postpone happiness until some time in the future. "Once Jim gets his promotion, then we'll have some time together" or "I know things will be better between us once I'm able to quit working outside the home."

That's all well and good, but if you are really serious about making your marriage all God intended it to be, you are going to have to stop postponing life. Instead, make the most of today, live it to the fullest. Not recklessly or foolishly, but savoring every moment. The wise man wrote, "…rejoice in the wife of your youth … may her breasts satisfy you always, may you ever be captivated by her love."[2] Notice the emphasis on "always" and "ever."

Some time ago, I was reminded of how important it is to live every moment of our lives when I read, "A Legacy of Rainbows" by Aletha Jane Lindstrom. She tells of pausing beside a park fountain one spring morning to watch the spray diffuse sunlight into shimmering rainbows. While she enjoyed the moment, a young mother, followed by a tiny blond girl, came hurrying along the path. "When the child saw the fountain, she threw her arms wide. 'Mommy, wait!' she cried. 'See all the pretty colors!'

"The mother reached for her daughter's hand. 'Come on,' she urged. 'We'll miss our bus!' Then seeing the joy on the small face, she relented. 'All right,' she said. 'There'll be another bus soon.'

"As she knelt with her arms around the child, joy filled the mother's face too, that rare and special joy of sharing something lovely with someone we love."[3]

There are moments like that in marriage too, and it is a wise couple who takes time to pause in the rush of living to savor them. Sometimes it's something as simple as a few bars of an old song or an especially beautiful sunset. At other times it may be a poignant moment as you face a family crisis like a beloved parent's open heart surgery, or the sorrow you share as you stand together beside the open grave of a loved one. Suddenly you know the true meaning of marriage, and you love each other so much you could cry.

ACTION STEPS

- Take a few minutes to examine your life right now. Are you living it to the fullest? Are you fully savoring every moment with your spouse, with your children? If you are not, ask yourself why.
- If you were to decide to live every moment to the fullest, what attitude adjustments would you have to make? What behavioral changes would be required? Be specific.

THOUGHT FOR THE DAY

"...the second memory is of the interior of our house when I happen to be home, once, and you are not. You've rearranged the furniture, and I stand gazing at the change you've made. I'm shaking my head. I'm shaking my head over you, astonished by your kindness. This house has two bedrooms; one is the children's, one is ours, and these are the only two rooms with doors and privacy. But here, in what used to be the sitting room, is all our bedroom furniture—and what used to be our bedroom has become a study, in which I am invited to write. Thanne! You've given up your bedroom. How can I answer that kind of love? I can't. I can only bow my head and stand in its light. And write."[4]

—Walter Wangerin, Jr.

SCRIPTURE FOR THE DAY

"You have stolen my heart, my sister, my bride; you have stolen my heart with one glance of your eyes, with one jewel of your necklace.

How delightful is your love, my sister, my bride!

How much more pleasing is your love than wine, and the fragrance of your perfume than any spice!

Your lips drop sweetness as the honeycomb, my bride; milk and honey are under your tongue.

The fragrance of your garments is like that of Lebanon."

—SONG OF SONGS 4:9-11

PRAYER

Lord, yesterday is past, and tomorrow may never come. This moment is all we have. Give us the wisdom and the courage to live it to the fullest. In the name of Jesus I pray. Amen.

NURTURE THE PROMISE OF TOMORROW

A third secret, Brenda and I have learned, for keeping romance in marriage is to nurture the promise of tomorrow. Even as we reminisce, cherishing the memories of yesterday—our first date, homecoming, our first apartment, Leah's birth—we are careful not to try to recapture those bygone days. That would be counterproductive. We are not the same people we were then. And what brought us such joy in our youth will not satisfy us now, nor should it. We use our past only as a way of enriching the present. And even as we look back, we also look ahead, knowing full well that how we live, and relate, today will determine the shape of our future.

We look forward to growing old together. We dream of one day retiring to a modest home in the Ozarks where I can write at my leisure. We fantasize about white Christmases, about Leah and her husband coming home with our grandbabies. And because the future is so precious, we dare not let love and romance be lost. Although we fully expect to be more in love twenty-five years from now, we know it won't just happen. To make that dream a reality, we will have to work at keeping romance in our marriage every day of our lives.

As Dr. James Dobson is so fond of saying: "Touching and talking and holding hands and gazing into one another's eyes and building memories are as important to partners in their midlife years as to rambunctious twenty-year-olds."[1]

For me, the essence of what I envision for our latter years is best summed up in an article by Phyllis Valkins called "A Kiss for Kate." She writes: "Every afternoon when I came on duty as the evening nurse, I would walk the halls of the nursing home, pausing at each door to chat and observe. Often, Kate and

Chris, their big scrapbooks in their laps, would be reminiscing over the photos. Proudly, Kate showed me pictures of bygone years: Chris tall, blonde, handsome. Kate pretty, dark-haired, laughing. Two young lovers smiling through the passing seasons. How lovely they looked now, sitting there, the light shining on their white heads, their time-wrinkled faces smiling at remembrances of the years, caught and held forever in the scrapbooks."[2]

Her conclusion? "How little the young know of loving. How foolish to think they have a monopoly on such a precious commodity. The old know what loving truly means; the young can only guess."[3]

For that vision to become a future reality, Brenda and I will have to seize every minute and not give it back until we have wrung every bit of life from it. And what is true for us is also true for you. If you don't savor the moment when it happens, you will miss it. If you try to go back and recapture it later, much of its magic will be gone; you will only hear a faint echo of your previous wonder. Remember, it will never happen quite like that again.

If you want to keep romance in your marriage, cherish the memories of the past, savor the joys of today and nurture the promise of tomorrow.

ACTION STEPS

- If your marriage were to continue on its present course for the next thirty, even forty years, what kind of relationship would you have? Would it be characterized by kindness and affection? Or would it be plagued by loneliness and bitterness? Remember, as you grow older, you do not necessarily change. In fact, most studies indicate that you will remain very much the way you are now only more so.
- Sit down with your spouse and visualize your retirement years, especially as it relates to your marriage relationship. Talk specifically about the kind of relationship you want to have in your later years. Decide together what changes, if any, you need to make in the way you relate to one another.

THOUGHT FOR THE DAY

"And the strongest trust is built by the smallest actions, the keeping of the little promises. It is the constant truthfulness, the continued dependability, the remembrance of minor things, which most inspire confidence and faith.

"O Thanne, that you might believe in my love during the desert days to come, I do this little thing, I make the bed this morning too. Then you will know me and wait for me, even when my soul is hidden from you."[4]

—Walter Wangerin, Jr.

SCRIPTURE FOR THE DAY

"I slept but my heart was awake.
    Listen! My lover is knocking:
'Open to me, my sister, my darling, my dove, my flawless one.
My head is drenched with dew, my hair with the dampness of the night.'
I have taken off my robe—must I put it on again?
I have washed my feet—must I soil them again?
My lover thrust his hand through the latch-opening; my heart began to pound for him.
I arose to open for my lover, and my hands dripped with myrrh, my fingers with flowing myrrh, on the handles of the lock.
I opened for my lover, but my lover had left; he was gone.
    My heart sank at his departure.
I looked for him but did not find him.
    I called him but he did not answer.
The watchmen found me as they made their rounds in the city.
They beat me, they bruised me; they took away my cloak, those watchmen of the walls!

O daughters of Jerusalem, I charge you—if you find my lover, what will you tell him?

Tell him I am faint with love."

—SONG OF SONGS 5:2-8

PRAYER

Lord, help us to realize that what we do today will become the material out of which we build our future. Unkind words, thoughtless deeds, broken promises, a trust betrayed, will become cornerstones in a house haunted by old hurts and present fears. Gentle words, acts of kindness, a promise kept, a love that is true, these are the cornerstones in the house built by love. May we never forget that the choices we make today will determine the house we live in tomorrow. In the name of Jesus I pray. Amen.

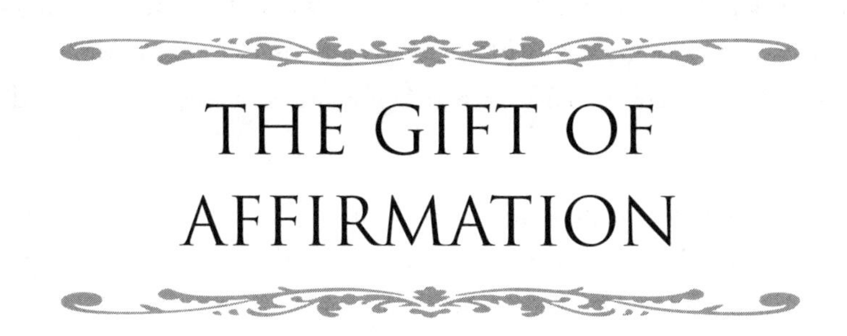

THE GIFT OF AFFIRMATION

No discussion regarding the keeping of romance in marriage would be complete without a reference to the gift of affirmation. It provides the climate in which romance can flourish. You should never assume that your wife knows how special you think she is. Tell her! Never assume that your husband knows you love him. Tell him! Remember, "...even the healthiest husbands and wives have enough doubts about themselves as persons worth loving to need regular affirmation from each other."[1]

Some years ago, while alone, on a ministry trip, I began reminiscing about the years Brenda and I have spent together. It was an incredible experience, and I ended up sharing many of my memories in a letter that I wrote to her. I could have called. It would have been far less trouble, but I would not have put the thought and effort into a call that I put into that letter. Besides, it would have been over in a matter of minutes. The letter she can keep for a lifetime.

With her permission, I would like to share parts of it with you here. I wrote: "Brenda, you really are an extraordinary person, not perfect, but definitely special.

"You are an unusually beautiful woman. We've been married almost twenty-eight years and I still light up when you walk into a room. I'm so proud to be seen with you. Without a doubt I look better when we're together.

"You are gracious and elegant. Under your touch leftovers become an occasion, and you can turn an ordinary drop-in evening into a festive event. You make cheese and crackers more elegant than caviar. What a joy to bring friends home to our house.

"Over the years, you have given me so much, more than I ever imagined possible. Simple things but rare—a quiet place away from the noisy world, a gentle love without demands, inspiration without expectations. Common things too, of uncommon value—a cup of coffee when I come home at night, a fire in the fireplace, supper on the stove.

"I give you me, now and always. I am yours in a way no one else can ever be yours, and in a way I can never be in relationship with anyone else. I will love you all the days of your life. When you are lonely I will comfort you. When you are tired I will refresh you. When you are sick I will care for you.

"I will share all your joys and sorrows your whole life long. We will celebrate growing old together, warmed against winter's chill, by the memories of a lifetime cherished and shared."

There's more, but I think you get the picture. When a husband and wife share their most tender feelings for one another, something almost miraculous happens. Their affirming words become light in a dark place, strength in a moment of weakness, music to the soul. And if their words are reinforced with tender gestures of affection, unexpected kindnesses and utter dependability, they experience a loving affirmation that enables them to embrace life in ways they never dared alone.

ACTION STEPS

- Take a few minutes right now and make a list of the things you most admire about your spouse. Look for opportune moments to share your admiration in the presence of family or friends, over a quiet lunch shared by just the two of you or even in the still of the night while you lie quietly waiting for sleep to come.
- Plan now to put your feelings on paper in the form of a love letter. Be sure to mail it rather than giving it to him/her personally. Somehow it seems to have more impact that way.

THOUGHT FOR THE DAY

"It is a wonder when your beloved trusts you enough to give herself to you again, trusts you with her weight, her treasure, and her life. In time the cup, which had proven itself, began to fill with the serious liquid of our lives. What a valuable vessel is a cup, a covenant!

"Now, though we may be separate in the morning, the ideas that occur to us apart we save for the hour when we will be together, because we trust in that hour; and it is as though we'd been together the whole day through. If Thanne suffers another sin of mine, it needn't swell in secret until it explodes. The cup is there for it, a place for it, and I drink from the cup, both the medicine that wakens and purges me, and the love with which she nourishes me."[2]

—Walter Wangerin, Jr.

SCRIPTURE FOR THE DAY

"How is your beloved better than others, most beautiful of women?
How is your beloved better than others, that you charge us so?
My lover is radiant and ruddy, outstanding among ten thousand.
His head is purest gold; his hair is wavy and black as a raven . . .
His mouth is sweetness itself; he is altogether lovely.
This is my lover, this my friend, O daughters of Jerusalem."

—Song of Songs 5:9-11,16

PRAYER

Lord, I thank You for those times when my beloved has spoken the words that enabled me to believe in myself again. Words that released me from the prison of doubt and insecurity, words that washed my wounds and healed my hurts, words that literally restored my life. Give me now, O Lord, I pray, this gift of affirmation that I might return to him/her the love and life he/she gave to me. In the name of Jesus I pray. Amen.

SEVEN

PREDICTABLE CRISES IN MARRIAGE

SECTION 7

PREDICTABLE CRISES IN MARRIAGE

"To speak of seasons is to say that the life course has a certain shape, that it evolves through a series of definable forms. A season is a relatively stable segment of the total cycle. Summer has a characteristic different from that of winter; twilight is different from sunrise. Just as there are seasons in our individual lives, so are there seasons in a marriage. To know these stages of development ahead of time is to be prepared for them."[1]

—H. Norman Wright

THE BIRTH OF THE FIRST CHILD

She loves her three-month-old baby, but she's exhausted. She loves her job, but she's exhausted.

She loves her husband, friends, parents, walking in the park, reading, gourmet cooking and having twenty minutes a week to herself, but she's exhausted.

It isn't supposed to be like this, at least not according to her way of thinking. She is not supposed to have moments when she resents her baby, her husband, everything. What happened to her idyllic vision of motherhood? You know, the one in which a young, model-perfect mom sings lullabies to her contented baby as she rocks him to sleep, while outside huge snowflakes drift down, creating a winter wonderland. Later, she will tuck him in his perfect baby bed before joining her husband in front of the fireplace for a quiet talk and some tender loving care.

But it is not at all like that for her. She has never been so tired in all her life. Her nights are a marathon of feedings and diapers and tiny, insufficient snatches of sleep. During the day she functions by rote, zombie-like, trying to maintain all of her pre-baby responsibilities, plus give her undivided attention to this little creature, who resembles nothing so much as a bottomless pit of needs. Somehow she manages, after a sort, though she cannot imagine how.

She is having a predictable marriage crisis—the birth of her first baby.

Her husband is experiencing a crisis of his own. Like his wife, he is thrilled and thankful for their baby, but nothing in the birthing classes prepared him for the drastic changes that have occurred in his life. His wife seems totally preoccupied with the baby. She never has time or energy for him, at least that's the way it seems. They never do anything together anymore. And, as crazy as it sounds, he almost feels jealous of his own child.

He's having a predictable marriage crisis—the birth of their first child.

According to H. Norman Wright, "Many family study experts say that the birth of the first child is a major crisis for many couples."[2] He adds, "Most couples have only a vague idea of what is entailed in the task of parenthood let alone the changes which occur in the marital relationship. One of the biggest adjustments is how to integrate this new person into the family so all three lives are enhanced."[3]

So, you may be wondering, how do we as a couple prepare for the birth of our first child? And once he's arrived, what can we do to minimize the stress while enhancing the joy?

Begin by being aware of what's happening. There is nothing wrong with you. Most new parents have a wide range of emotional reactions, especially the first few months. They feel absolutely euphoric joy and, in turn, unbelievable resentment. They also have moments when they feel overwhelmed by the awesome responsibilities of parenting.

Well do I remember the joy radiating from Ron and Charlene's faces when I visited them in the hospital a few hours after their first child was born. In spite of the fact that the delivery had been difficult, they were still awed by it all. For them, the miracle of birth was a deeply spiritual experience, one that left them profoundly moved. With parental pride they presented their newborn daughter for my inspection. Ron took out his camera and insisted that I allow him to photograph me holding the baby.

Equally well do I remember Ron's telephone call a week or so after they had taken the baby home. He was at his wit's end. Sleeplessness and stress had rubbed his emotions raw. Tearfully he confessed, "Pastor, this is not at all like I expected. All this baby does is eat and sleep and poop. And cry! Boy, can she cry!"

Hesitantly he continued, shame making his voice almost inaudible, "I don't think I love her. I almost wish she wasn't here."

He paused then, waiting, I think, for my rebuke. Instead, I shared the details of Brenda's struggle to accept Leah. Her delivery was also difficult, leaving Brenda exhausted and riddled with pain. Then she suffered a major hemorrhage and had to have emergency surgery to save her life. During her recovery she had little or no desire to see or hold her baby. Later she told me that she couldn't help blaming Leah for all that had happened to her. Of course, her feelings passed, and her love for Leah was now something to behold.

After hearing this account, Ron felt better. Just knowing that he wasn't the only parent who had such feelings helped, but the clincher was the relationship Brenda and Leah now shared. Their closeness is obvious to all. Their relationship goes beyond the normal mother/daughter thing. They are also the best of friends. By the time we said good-bye, Ron had every confidence that his negative feelings would pass, to be replaced by the love of a father for his daughter.

It also helps to realize that the initial draining schedule of a newborn does not last forever. Things will get better. See the child for who he is, a person in his own right. He is not a sexual rival or a substitute for either spouse.

Finally, develop flexibility in meeting your spouse's needs. Expanding the ability to express frustrations and feelings, and even delaying some need-satisfaction, will be a major step toward restoring marital understanding and closeness.

ACTION STEPS

- If you are preparing for your first child, talk with some friends who have already had a baby. Ask them what kind of changes it made in their daily habits and in their relationship. Seek their advice regarding the adjustments you will likely have to make.
- If you have just had your first child, use this material as a basis for discussing what's happening in your relationship. Honestly share your feelings, both positive and negative, but remember to be careful not to attack your spouse. Even if you can't change anything, talking about it often relieves stress, even as it enables you to reconnect with your spouse.

THOUGHT FOR THE DAY

"We spend many years preparing for our vocation and in some instances work into it gradually. We spend six months to four years becoming acquainted with our spouse prior to marriage and this relationship gradually grows and develops. Not so with parenthood! We are aware that the child is coming, and then abruptly a minute later—this new stranger is alive, loud and demanding."[4]

—H. Norman Wright

SCRIPTURES FOR THE DAY

"The father of a righteous man has great joy; he who has a wise son delights in him.
May your father and mother be glad; may she who gave you birth rejoice!"

—PROVERBS 23:24,25

"Sons are a heritage from the Lord, children a reward from him.
Like arrows in the hands of a warrior are sons born in one's youth.
Blessed is the man whose quiver is full of them...."

—PSALM 127:3-5

PRAYER

Lord, I dedicate my son/daughter to You. I pray that You will protect him/her from accident and injury. Take sickness and disease from him/her. Give him/her a heart that hungers and thirsts for righteousness, eyes that look with compassion upon the needy, hands that touch and heal, and a desire ever to do Your eternal will. Fulfill Your purposes in his/her life. In the name of Jesus I pray. Amen.

THE SEVEN-YEAR ITCH[1]

Poet Lois Wyse graphically describes the second predictable crisis in marriage. In a poem titled "Words for a Five-Star Loser" she writes:

"I met a famous man at a dinner party the other night,
and I extended my hand and said,
'I'm one of your admirers. I've read a lot about you.
And he stood up and said,
'You've probably read about my five marriages, too.'
I hadn't, except for the famous early headline ones.
'Trouble with me,' he said, 'is this…
Every time I fall in love I get married.
No marriage lasted more than ten years.
Around seven years I get itchy.'
Look, famous man, sit down, and let me tell you something.
Around seven years everybody gets itchy.
Dumb executives and smart plumbers and wives.
Oh, do wives get itchy.
They get itchy putting up hems and taking down storm windows.
They get itchy when they go to the movies or watch TV.
They get itchy making hamburger patties
  And diapering bottoms
  And holding heads.
They get itchy
Putting children to bed and getting husbands up.
They get itchy
Just thinking about men like you getting itchy.
That's the itchiest feeling of all."[2]

At the risk of offending you, let me add that along about seven years into marriage Christian husbands and wives get itchy too. In *Seasons of a Marriage,* H. Norman Wright says, "...research indicates that at least one-half of those married will have at least one affair. And it is totally naive to believe that it is just the non-Christians who become involved. Almost all the couples I know or have seen in counseling who have been involved in affairs are Christians. They seem to have one unique characteristic, however. I believe they delay going for help longer than non-Christians; also they are more secretive about their affairs."[3]

Am I saying that an affair is inevitable about seven years into marriage? Absolutely not! I am, however, saying that temptation is inevitable, and it is crucial that we prepare for it. To use an old adage: "To be forewarned is to forearmed."

The first step in preventing an affair is to understand how and why marital infidelity occurs. Contrary to popular belief, most affairs begin for nonsexual reasons. The lack of need fulfillment and intimacy creates an intense vacuum, making the desire for emotional intimacy the primary reason why people have an extramarital affair. Many a shocked husband has said, after discovering that his wife is having an affair, "What does she see in him?" His wife's response? "He listens, cares and he doesn't criticize me!"

Don't misunderstand me. I am not excusing infidelity. There are no extenuating circumstances, no situations where adultery can be justified. I mention emotional deprivation as a warning signal only. When the need for closeness, goodness, kindness and togetherness—what I call our "ness" needs—is not being met on a regular basis in a marriage, the temptation may be to find a person who will be good to us, touch us, hold us, give us a feeling of closeness. Sexual fulfillment may, indeed, become an important part of an extramarital relationship, but the "ness" needs are, for most men and women, initially more important.

Dr. Carlfred Broderick, successful marriage counselor and author, has talked to dozens of couples who have been fully committed to fidelity, yet found themselves involved in affairs. He says: "I am convinced that more people get themselves into the pain of infidelity through empathy, concern and compassion than through any base motive. The world is full of lonely and vulnerable people, hungry for a sympathetic ear and a shoulder to cry on."[4]

What am I trying to say? Simply this: An innocent get-together like working on a project, helping a neighbor or even meeting for coffee, can begin a pattern of meetings that become increasingly mutually fulfilling. Soon the parties are sharing deeply, which gives birth to emotional intimacy, which, inexorably leads to adultery. Or as one man put it, "In two weeks we were in bed together. I just can't believe it's happening to me!"

It is crucial that we end the relationship before that emotional bond forms. Should we fail to do so, the power of passion takes over, distorting reality and rendering us incapable of making spiritually sound decisions.

It is important to establish simple guidelines regarding appropriate boundaries for our relationships before we are tempted to stray. For instance, experience has taught me that I should not form a close friendship with a member of the opposite sex; it's simply too dangerous. Rigid? Perhaps, but hardly when one considers the tragedies befalling so many couples.

Even as a couple, building a relationship with another couple, we must make a conscious effort to maintain appropriate boundaries. Not infrequently a special friendship ends in adultery. Where does a relationship get off track? That's hard to pinpoint. "A situation like that develops very subtly. The process is usually so complex and deceptive that it is frequently impossible, even in retrospect, to pinpoint a single event or point in time when 'it happened.'"[5]

Two boundaries that must be carefully guarded are in the areas of personal conversation and physical contact. Dr. Richard Dobbins, founder and director of Emerge Ministries, writes, "As friendships among couples grow more intimate, there is a tendency to become too personal and permissive in discussing the sexual side of life.... When personal boundaries are ignored over a long period of time, the frequency and intimacy of contacts allowed between close friends can threaten to lead the best intentioned person to an emotional 'point of no return' which can be disastrous."[6]

For others the journey into the spiritual and emotional pitfalls of adultery begins with some "innocent flirting" that is carefully couched in double meanings. If the one being flirted with fails to respond, or becomes offended, the person doing the flirting can protest his innocence, claiming he was misunderstood. On the other hand, if the "flirtee" responds in kind, the chase is on, and excitement is high. Neither person has yet made a conscious decision to commit adultery, but subconsciously they are committed to it.

Once this deadly descent begins, it rapidly advances from one stage to the next. The potential adulterers spend significant amounts of time fantasizing about each other. As the "affair" progresses, these fantasies become more explicit. For the man they will often be sexual in nature, though not always; while for the woman they will usually be romantic.

During the next stage they find excuses for calling each other. And they will spend extended periods of time in deep conversations—often about spiritual things or personal problems. They will create legitimate reasons for spending time together—a special church project or choir program—anything that allows them to be with one another.

By this time they are actively committing adultery, not physically, but emotionally; that is, they are getting their "ness" needs met by someone other than their spouse. Someone other than their spouse is satisfying their need for closeness, tenderness and togetherness.

Now they begin to justify their relationship. First, they carefully catalog every failure in their marriage. They recite their spouse's shortcomings in deadly detail. They remember and magnify every problem. Their spouse is insensitive and unresponsive. Surely God doesn't expect them to live their entire lives in such an unhappy state. With a little help from such rationalization their compatibility leads smoothly into tenderness, the tenderness to a need for privacy, the privacy to physical consolation, and the consolation straight to bed.

Once they physically commit adultery, they find themselves in a maelstrom of emotions. Guilt and fear haunt them. Their self-esteem falters. They live with the constant fear of being found out. Prayer seems impossible. How can they face God? Yet even as they writhe in remorse, they are driven with excitement and desire. They hate what they are doing, but they feel powerless to stop. They vow to break it off, to go back to just being friends, but to no avail. Their good intentions are just that—good intentions—nothing more. Like moths drawn irresistibly to a flame, they seem destined to self-destruct.

As the affair progresses, their excitement wears off, while their guilt and fear increase. Now they feel trapped. There is no way out of the relationship without hurting the other person, yet they can't continue like this indefinitely either. No matter what they do now, someone is going to get hurt and hurt bad!

Now they must face the spouse they have betrayed and the children they have abandoned and the God they have disobeyed. The consequences of their sin will reverberate through eternity, hurting the innocent as certainly as the guilty. The consequences are inevitable:

> "Can a man scoop fire into his lap
> without his clothes being burned?
> Can a man walk on hot coals
> without his feet being scorched?
> So is he who sleeps with another man's wife;
> no one who touches her will go unpunished ...
> a man who commits adultery lacks judgment;
> whoever does so destroys himself.
> Blows and disgrace are his lot,
> and his shame will never be wiped away."[7]

If you've caught a glimpse of your relationship as you've read this, now is the time to take corrective action. Give your marriage first priority. Invest time and energy in the relationship. Determine to meet each other's "ness" needs. If you don't know where to start, seek competent help from a minister or a Christian marriage counselor. Your marriage is worth whatever it takes to make it all it can be.

ACTION STEPS

- Study the five early warning signals listed below. Invite the Holy Spirit to examine your heart and your relationships in light of these insights.

  1) **A growing fascination with a person of the opposite sex other than your spouse.** Beware when he/she regularly intrudes upon your thoughts, even when you are with your spouse and family.

  2) **A heightened sense of anticipation when you have an opportunity to be with him/her.** Beware when you find yourself looking forward to those "ministry" opportunities when you can legitimately be alone with him/her, or when you volunteer for church projects so the two of you can be together.

3) **A growing desire to confide in him/her.** Beware when you are tempted to share with him/her the frustrations and disappointments in your own marriage.

4) **An increased sense of responsibility for his/her happiness and well-being.** Beware when you think more about his/her needs than the needs of your own spouse and family.

5) **Emotional distancing from your spouse.** Beware when you have an increasing need to keep your thoughts and feelings for him/her secret from your spouse.

- If there is anything dangerous or inappropriate about any relationship in your life, confess it to God and renounce it. Terminate the friendship immediately and make yourself accountable to a trusted friend or to your pastor.

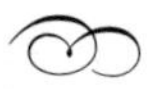

THOUGHT FOR THE DAY

"Men, put disciplined hedges around your life—especially if you work with women. Refrain from verbal intimacy with women other than your spouse. Do not bare your heart to another woman, or pour forth your troubles to her. Intimacy is a great need in most people's lives—and talking about personal matters, especially one's problems, can fill another's need of intimacy, awakening a desire for more. Many affairs begin in just this way.

"On the practical level, do not touch. Do not treat women with the casual affection you extend to females in your family. How many tragedies have begun with brotherly or fatherly touches and then sympathetic shoulders. You may have to run the risk of being wrongly considered 'distant' or 'cold' by some women.

"Never flirt—even in jest. Flirtation is intrinsically flattering. You may think you are being cute, but it often arouses unrequited desires in another."[8]

—R. Kent Hughes

SCRIPTURE FOR THE DAY

"Another thing you do: You flood the Lord's altar with tears. You weep and wail because he no longer pays attention to your offerings or accepts them with pleasure from your hands. You ask, 'Why?' It is because the Lord is acting as the witness between you and the wife of your youth, because you have broken faith with her, though she is your partner, the wife of your marriage covenant.

"Has not the Lord made them one? In flesh and spirit they are his. And why one? Because he was seeking godly offspring. So guard yourself in your spirit, and do not break faith with the wife of your youth.

"'I hate divorce,' says the Lord God of Israel, 'and I hate a man's covering himself with violence as well as with his garment,' says the Lord Almighty.

"So guard yourself in your spirit, and do not break faith."

—MALACHI 2:13-16

PRAYER

Lord, it is not so much evil as emptiness that makes us susceptible to sexual sin. Therefore I ask You to make me especially sensitive to my spouse's emotional needs. Give me the special ability needed to fully satisfy his/her "ness" needs. And make him/her, I pray, especially sensitive to my needs as well. Enable him/her, by the power of Your Holy Spirit, to meet all of my "ness" needs. Build a hedge around our marriage. Protect our hearts from the evil one. In Jesus' name I pray. Amen.

THE EMPTY NEST

Roy and Linda had been married nearly thirty years when their third child, and only daughter, was married in a beautiful wedding, flawlessly choreographed by Linda. As that eventful day wound to a close, Linda's father sought her out. "It was perfect," he said, "from beginning to end." She gave him a wan smile, before taking his hand and leading him to an empty bench.

When they were both seated, he asked, "Is something wrong, Linda?"

Blinking rapidly to keep back her tears, she said, "For the past year I've been consumed with planning Lori's wedding. It's been my life, you might say. But now..." Her voice trailed off.

"What are you trying to say, Linda?" her father asked anxiously.

"Oh, Daddy," she sounded like a little girl again as she let him hug her while she wept soundlessly.

When she had regained composure, she tried again: "Things aren't the way they used to be. Between Roy and me, I mean. And now that it's just the two of us, I don't know what I'm going to do. I don't think I can hide from the truth any longer."

"Have you talked with Roy ... about this, I mean?"

"I've tried, Daddy, but he gets that hurt little boy look on his face, and I can't go on. He seems to be so happy, and I don't want to shatter his world." Taking a deep breath she continued, "I thought I could manage it, and I did pretty well as long as Lori was at home, but now that she's leaving I don't know what I'm going to do."

Linda's experience is not uncommon, more acute than most couples' experience, perhaps, but common nonetheless. When the last child leaves home, or gets married, the dynamics of family life change radically. Needs for communication, affection and companionship that were once filled, at least in part, by the children must now be met by someone else. Suddenly, a man and his wife are thrown together with no one else to talk to. It's a grand opportunity for intimacy, but for many couples it's threatening. The empty nest becomes a major crisis when two strangers suddenly find themselves alone with each other with the rest of their lives stretching out in front of them.

It's called a predictable crisis because we know it is going to happen. As surely as children are born, they will grow up and leave the nest. It is part of God's divine plan. Still, that does not make it painless. Under the best of circumstances, it is challenging. Under less than ideal circumstances, it can become a crisis.

It becomes a major crisis when the only thing a couple has in common is their children. The wife who invests herself in the children to the exclusion of a relationship with her husband is at high risk come midlife. Likewise, the man who involves himself in his career to such a degree that he has no time or energy left for his wife. One mother, who experienced this "post-parental depression," said she felt like dying when her last daughter got married.

Preparing for the empty nest is not complicated, but it is demanding. Nothing is more essential than maintaining an intimate relationship with each other. Private time and deep sharing should be cultivated at all costs. He must guard against becoming over involved in his career, and she must be careful not to invest so much of herself in the children that there is nothing left for each other.

Be careful not to live as if your children will be with you always. They won't. As they grow up and become increasingly independent, experience your own independence. The empty nest is really a progressive thing. As your children make a few short solo flights, go ahead and deal with your feelings. Don't store them all up for one big crisis.

Accept your new role rather than grieving over the one you've lost. Your value as a person has not diminished, just changed. Strive to relate to your children as an adult to an adult, rather than as a parent to a child. Those who manage this soon discover a rewarding new relationship. They haven't lost a child, they have gained a new friend. The empty nest, like the other predictable crises in marriage, can be an opportunity for enrichment. It's what you make it. The choice is yours.

ACTION STEPS

Your children will grow up and leave home. You will eventually retire from your job. Marriage is the only relationship in your life that is until "death do us part." Does not wisdom, then, dictate that you invest yourself in your marriage whatever the cost? Examine your life and list the behaviors that give evidence that you are preparing for that day when it will only be the two of you.

THOUGHT FOR THE DAY

"Many studies show that when the last child grows up and leaves home there is an increased likelihood of marital maladjustment. This event acts as a marital catalyst, demanding that the husband and wife face themselves, each other, and their marriage in a new way. The longer they avoid this task, the faster the gap between them widens."[1]

—H. Norman Wright

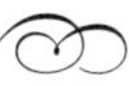

SCRIPTURE FOR THE DAY

"Blessed are all who fear the Lord, who walk in his ways.

You will eat the fruit of your labor; blessings and prosperity will be yours.

Your wife will he like a fruitful vine within your house; your sons will be like olive shoots around your table.

Thus is the man blessed who fears the Lord."

—PSALM 128:1-4

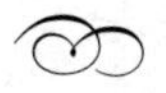

PRAYER

Lord, life is so fleeting. Only yesterday, it seems, we were bringing our baby home for the first time. Now he/she is growing up and soon will be leaving us to begin a life of his/her own. Then it will be just the two of us again. The future is a little frightening, but I'm excited too, Lord. Bless our union, I pray, and may our latter years be even more blessed than our former years. In the name of Jesus I pray. Amen.

MIDLIFE CRISIS[1]

"The midlife crisis," according to author Jim Conway, "is a time of high risk for marriages. It's a time of possible career disruption and extramarital affairs. There is depression, anger, frustration and rebellion. The crisis is a pervasive thing that seems to affect not only the physical but also the social, cultural, spiritual and occupational expressions of a man's life."[2]

One of the reasons midlife is so hard on a marriage is because a role reversal often occurs: "Men tend to move toward passivity, tenderness and intimacy which they previously repressed. They move toward more expressive ventures and goals. Women tend to become more autonomous, aggressive and cognitive. They now seek more instrumental roles such as a career, money, influence."[3] In short, at the mid-point in their lives husbands and wives are moving in opposite directions and often miss each other, passing like ships in the night.

This role reversal, and the resulting crisis, often indicates a weakness in the way many couples relate to their careers and their families. It underlines the futility of a one-dimensional life. The man has invested himself in his career at the expense of his relationship with his family and friends. At midlife he realizes how unsatisfying that is, and he can't imagine spending the rest of his days so unfulfilled. The woman, on the other hand, has been a caregiver, nurturing her children and to some degree her husband. Even as he is discovering that his career cannot meet all of his emotional needs, she is beginning to realize that living through her family only is not enough either, especially now that the children are grown. In a misguided effort to make a new identity, she often moves away from her husband in search of independence just when he is turning toward her in search of intimacy. The result—a marriage-threatening midlife crisis.

Can it be avoided? I think so. Midlife will always present challenges, but it does not have to be a time of crisis. The key to preventing a crisis is concomitant growth. The man or woman who leads a one-dimensional life is at greater risk than the person who invests himself or herself in a number of areas. The main cause of a midlife crisis is the threat to personal identity. Those who sail through this period without apparent trauma are those who have built a varied and solid identity. They see themselves in several roles—spouse, parent, friend, professional, and as a person in his or her own right. Should one of these roles or identities be threatened, they are not devastated. They know they are more than just an "accountant" or just a "parent."

In addition, they are expressive persons. They are in touch with their humanity and are willing to share their deepest feelings with those they know and trust. This enables them to establish a social and emotional network, a support system, in which they are helped to process their feelings as they occur, rather than denying them for years and then suddenly having to deal with them all at once.

And finally, they are persons who have incorporated the Word of God into their lives. Their confidence is not in temporal things like physical appearance or strength, material wealth or position. They are grounded in the eternal values of God's Word, and, as a consequence, they cannot only negotiate change, but thrive on it.

ACTION STEPS

- If you are between the ages of thirty-five and fifty-five, take an emotional inventory of your life. Do you feel trapped, used, unfulfilled, overwhelmed or some similar emotion? Take a few minutes and write out a detailed description of your feelings.
- Now process these feelings with someone you trust—your spouse, your pastor or a friend. The experience of sharing your feelings often makes them less overwhelming and more manageable. Pray about these issues together.
- As a couple, discuss lifestyle changes that will decrease the risk of a marriage-threatening midlife crisis. Take specific steps to implement those changes now.

THOUGHT FOR THE DAY

"I believe that middle-aged marriage, lived as it should be and can be, offers qualities that nothing else has ever superseded: A shelter where two people can grow older without loneliness, the ease of long intimacy, family jokes that don't have to be explained, understanding without words. Most of all it offers memories."[4]

—M. Brown

SCRIPTURE FOR THE DAY

"There is a time for everything, and a season for every activity under heaven: a time to be born and a time to die, a time to plant and a time to uproot, a time to kill and a time to heal, a time to tear down and a time to build, a time to weep and a time to laugh, a time to mourn and a time to dance, a time to scatter stones and a time to gather them, a time to embrace and a time to refrain, a time to search and a time to give up, a time to keep and a time to throw away, a time to tear and a time to mend, a time to be silent and a time to speak, a time to love and a time to hate, a time for war and a time for peace."

—ECCLESIASTES 3:1-8

PRAYER

Lord, change is never easy, especially when it means growing older, seeing our children leave home, and watching our beloved parents age and die. Yet, it is an inevitable fact of life, and those who make peace with it find a joy that escapes everyone else. Grant us, now, the grace to make peace with midlife and all it brings. Give us faith to believe that this season, too, can be a time of personal and spiritual growth. Teach us to live all the days of our life and to love each other more through the passing seasons. In the name of Jesus I pray. Amen.

THE DEATH OF A SPOUSE[1]

The final predictable crisis in marriage is the death of a spouse. Joe Bayly describes death as "a wound to the living."[2] That, I think, characterizes it best, especially for the Christian. Death separates you from the people you love best, and in the case of a spouse's death, from the person you loved best. You are comforted by the knowledge that your beloved is with the Lord, and with the thought that you will be reunited with him/her one day, but that does not alleviate the awful pain you experience following his/her death. The one you've loved and lived with for a lifetime is suddenly taken from you, leaving a gaping hole in your heart.

In the days and weeks immediately following the death of your spouse, you will experience a terrible grief. You will live with the desolation of a hauntingly empty house that, not so long ago, resounded to the joyous laughter of your beloved. You will learn to eat alone at the table in the sunlit breakfast nook where the two of you so often enjoyed the quiet of early morning and talked of growing old together. You will be painfully reminded of your aloneness, and your loss, each time something—a few bars of a favorite song, a phone call from a friend, an old snapshot—reminds you of a shared experience. Only now you have no one to share your feelings with.

I remember one grieving widower telling me that the hardest thing for him to bear was those times when something interesting or funny happened and he would think, *I must remember to tell this to Margaret.* Then he would be reminded that Margaret was dead. At such times his grief was nearly unbearable.

Because grief is so painful, you may be tempted to seek not only relief, but escape. Don't! While that reaction is not unusual, it is counterproductive. As painful as your grief is, it is not a foe to be overcome, but a friend to be embraced. If you insist on thinking of your grief as an enemy, you will only delay the healing process. You may deny your grief, even repress it for a time, but you cannot escape it. One way or the other, you will grieve! The only real choice you have is how and when.

Grief itself is painful, but not injurious. It is a wound that brings healing in much the same way that a proper surgical procedure wounds the body in order to heal it. As C.S. Lewis wrote in a letter to a dear friend whose wife had died: "...I am sure it is never sadness—a proper, straight, natural response to loss—that does people harm, but all the other things, all the resentment, dismay, doubt and self-pity with which it is usually complicated."[3]

It may be helpful to remember that your beloved was a gift from God, pure and simple. He/she was never really yours, not in the sense that we tend to think. You were privileged to enjoy life with him/her for a time ... and now he/she is gone. You can hold that against God and grow bitter, or you can thank God that you were given the gift of his/her presence for a time, however short.

If you choose to thank God for what you had, rather than to blame Him for what you have lost, I believe you will discover a new dimension of life. That doesn't mean that you won't grieve, or that you won't miss him/her. Rather, it means that not even death can rob you of the joys you shared together! Nor can it steal the hope of the present or the promise of the future. The God who makes all things new is now present to renew your life. He wants to give you the grace to enjoy living again!

While the severity of the initial shock will diminish, the grief itself will last somewhere between eighteen and thirty-six months. As time passes, your grief will slowly recede. It can be likened to the tide which comes in and goes out. As the days turn into weeks and then months, you will notice the tide of grief staying out longer and longer. And when it does come rolling in again, it is not with such severity. One day you will discover that you are thinking of your departed spouse without pain. The life you shared, with its memories, good and bad, has finally replaced the omnipresent memory of his or her death. Now your grief work is almost done.

During the initial stages though, you may think you are losing your mind as you experience a host of violent emotions. These include, but are not necessarily limited to, shock and crying, guilt, hostility and restless activity. Realizing that these feelings are normal and necessary can be a tremendous help in facilitating the grief process.

During your time of grief you will need a safe place, preferably your own home. Some grieving people prefer to withdraw because their home reminds them of loss; but giving up your home and moving only creates more of a loss. A brief change may be all right, but familiar surroundings are more helpful.

If possible, surround yourself with safe people—friends, relatives and a minister. They are necessary in order to provide the emotional support you need. (If you are ministering to a bereaved person, it is better to visit the person four times a week for ten minutes than once a week for an hour. This provides more continual support without becoming exhausting.)

It is also important to involve yourself in safe situations. Anything that provides you with a worthwhile role to perform is beneficial. These situations should be uncomplicated and simple, and should not create anxiety.

Of course, it is critically important that you give yourself permission to complete your grief work. Grief work is the reviewing of your life together with the deceased. This involves thinking about him/her; remembering dates, events, happy times and special occasions; looking at photos; and handling trophies or items important to him/her. In a sense, all of these activities are involved in the process of psychologically burying the dead.

Since grief makes your friends uncomfortable, they may have a tendency to deny you the opportunity to do your grief work. They may come into your home and find you crying as you look at old pictures of the two of you together. If so, they will likely say, "Let's go do something else and get your mind off of this." If you can, resist the temptation to comply. Instead, invite them to share the painful memories with you.

In the final stages of your grief work, you will find yourself embracing life again. Instead of always remembering what once was, you will find yourself considering the future. At first you may feel guilty, as if you are being disloyal to his/her memory. Of course, you are not, but it may feel that way just the same. This too is part of the process of emancipating yourself from the deceased in order to begin building new relationships and attachments.

Rabbi Joshua Liebman, in his book *Peace of Mind,* wrote an excellent chapter on grief's slow wisdom, which speaks most eloquently to the temptation not to return to normal activities. Liebman said, "The melody that the loved one played upon the piano of your life will never be played quite that way again, but we must not close the keyboard and allow the instrument to gather dust. We must seek out other artists of the spirit, new friends who gradually will help us to find the road to life again, who will walk that road with us."[4]

Remember, there is life after death, here and in the hereafter.

ACTION STEPS

Although the death of your spouse may seem inconceivable to you at this stage of your life, let me encourage you to consider it. Have the two of you considered such things as life insurance and a will? Are both of you fully informed regarding your family finances? Take some time and discuss what to do in case either of you should die.

Make a detailed list of things to do in the event that one of you should die. Your list should include: 1) funeral arrangements and place of burial, 2) a list of life insurance policies and their location, 3) a detailed list of assets and liabilities, and 4) the name of a trusted friend or financial advisor.

THOUGHTS FOR THE DAY

"Although the ultimate reality of heaven is beyond our comprehension, God has revealed the essence of it. And always that essence is of a far grander scale than anything this earthly life affords. That being the case, how can we doubt that our most intimate earthly relationships will not be somehow enhanced in heaven? I agree with C.S. Lewis who said, 'I think the union between the risen spouses will be as close as that between the soul and its own risen body.'"[5]

—Richard Exley

"As surely as day follows the night, As surely as winter yields to spring, so shall the chilling seasons of grief, give way to the fullness of life."

—Richard Exley

SCRIPTURE FOR THE DAY

"'Lord,' Martha said to Jesus, 'if you had been here, my brother would not have died. But I know that even now God will give you whatever you ask.'

"Jesus said to her, 'Your brother will rise again.'

"Martha answered, 'I know he will rise again in the resurrection at the last day.'

"Jesus said to her, 'I am the resurrection and the life. He who believes in me will live, even though he dies; and whoever lives and believes in me will never die. Do you believe this?'

"'Yes, Lord,' she told him, 'I believe that you are the Christ, the Son of God, who was to come into the world.'"

—JOHN 11:21-27

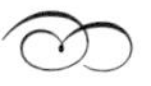

PRAYER

Lord, teach us to live all the days of our life so that when death comes we will have no regrets. Let us speak every endearing word that fills our heart. Let us express all the love and affection that we feel, holding nothing back. Don't let us withhold a single affirming word, or even the smallest gesture of affection. Let us share all of our love all the days of our lives. In the name of Jesus I pray. Amen.

EIGHT

The Healing of a Broken Marriage

SECTION 8

THE HEALING OF A BROKEN MARRIAGE

"The problem with being bitter and resentful is that we have allowed what our spouse has said or done to control our emotions and our lives. If we do not release our spouse from whatever wrong he or she has done, we simply enslave ourselves to the hurt in our past. Being chained to hurt and hate from the past means anger and resentment in our future. When we hold onto our hurts we are misusing the gift of memory. We are choosing to use our memory to hurt as we have been hurt. How? By keeping the hurt alive and in some way perhaps plotting to hurt in return. We use memory as a weapon."[1]

"Forgiveness is not a feeling. It is not a soothing, comforting, overwhelming emotional response that erases the fact from our memory. It is a clear and logical action that does not bring up the past offenses and hurts but takes each day a step at a time. Gradually there will be a bit less anger and resentment and a bit more forgiveness until eventually there is a wholeness once again."[2]

—H. Norman Wright

THINGS THAT WOUND

Unfortunately, even the best marriages suffer wounds. Sooner or later we all sin against our mate, our marriage and our love. Sometimes our sins are deliberate and premeditated, but more often than not we sin against our marriage without giving it a thought. We sin carelessly, out of ignorance or indifference rather than cruelty. Whatever the motivation, or the circumstances, our sins will wound our spouse and our marriage. Unresolved, they will eventually precipitate a crisis.

"You think you know me, but you don't!" Esther spit the words out.

After a tense moment her husband replied, "I guess I don't, but God knows I've tried. How you can blame me for not knowing you when you deliberately disguise your real feelings is beyond me."

"Dale," she said, anger giving way to a tired sadness, "you don't want to know me. You want to control me. You want to tell me what to think and how to feel."

When he still seemed baffled, she tried again. "You run my whole life, and you have for thirty years. The only part of me that is mine is what I keep from you."

As a pastor I found their situation especially sad. They were both Christians and leaders in the church, yet after thirty years of marriage Esther had found herself involved with another man. Things came to a head when she confessed her infidelity and sought Dale's forgiveness. Now, together, we were trying to restore their broken marriage.

Although her affair had not been premeditated, in retrospect it seems almost inevitable. Dale was a good man, but as she said, a controlling one, and very much like her father in that respect. As a child, Esther had learned to say and do what was expected of her in order to win her father's approval and escape his discipline.

On the inside, though, she had lived a secret life with her own ideas and values. When she married, she simply transferred this unhealthy way of coping to her relationship with her husband.

To complicate matters, Dale was a volatile man given to outbursts of anger, which only made Esther more determined to avoid a confrontation. He was not a mean man, and his verbal outbursts were always followed by sincere apologies. Over the years, though, his anger had taken its toll. Although Esther could not confront him, her resentment had kept building until she concluded that she did not love him, indeed could not love him.

Even then, there was no thought of divorce, or infidelity. She simply decided to find her fulfillment in other areas—her children, her friends and her work. Fearing confrontation above all else, she was careful to hide her hurt and loneliness from her husband. She continued to perform her wifely duties as if she was not dying on the inside. Self-centered, as such men are wont to be, Dale never noticed a thing.

When circumstances thrust her into a working relationship with Brad, she found herself enjoying his company in a way she had never enjoyed being with her husband. Brad respected her opinions and never tried to tell her what to think. For the first time in her life, she was with a man who did not try to dominate her. With Brad she felt safe, safe enough to be her real self.

Of course, it was only a matter of time until she and Brad were confiding in each other, which created an emotional bond, which in turn led to sexual intimacy. Both Esther and Brad were married, and they were both Christians. They hated what they were doing, but seemed powerless to stop. On several occasions they vowed to end their infidelity, to return to just being friends, only to discover that once the barriers to intimacy have been breached they are almost impossible to restore. Because they worked together, it was impossible to terminate the relationship completely without creating a financial hardship, not to mention the risk of explaining such a decision.

Brad and Esther continued in their self-made trap for several months. Finally, she could bear her guilt no more and in desperation confessed everything to her husband. She fully expected it to end their marriage. Even if Dale did not demand a divorce, she knew that she could not live the rest of her life a prisoner of his anger. To Esther's fearful surprise he wanted to forgive her and restore their marriage. It was a fearful thing because she did not want to fall back into the trap that her marriage had become. She did not want to spend the rest of her days in a loveless marriage in which she had to pretend to be something she was not in order to be accepted by her husband.

It was a fearful thing for Dale too. He wondered if he could ever trust her again. Could he change? Could he learn to control his verbal outbursts? Could he accept her as a person in her own right and not just as an extension of himself? Could she learn to express her real feelings even at the risk of a confrontation? Could their marriage really be restored? These and a thousand other questions tormented him day and night. In desperation the two of them decided to seek my pastoral counsel.

The real problem was not infidelity, but the unhealthy ways they related to each other. Healing the wounds caused by Esther's affair would, in many ways, be easier than changing the way they interacted with each other. Esther had to overcome a lifetime of conditioning. Her father would tolerate no dissenting opinion, consequently she had learned early in life to be passive-aggressive. In marrying a man much like her father, Esther had continued her unhealthy way of relating. She enjoyed the security of being married to a man who "took care of things," but she hated feeling controlled. In order to heal her marriage, Esther had to learn to express her feelings early on before they became infected with bitterness and resentment. It wouldn't be easy because it might precipitate a confrontation requiring her to validate her feelings, both for herself, and for her husband.

For his part, Dale had to trust her enough to allow her to come to her own conclusions. His attempts to control her were really evidence of a lack of trust. He feared she would not make spiritually and emotionally sound decisions. Yet, if Dale and Esther were truly to relate as husband and wife, he had to stop behaving like her father. It wouldn't be easy because the father/daughter dynamic, though terribly unfulfilling, was a role to which they both had become accustomed.

How different things might have been had either of them recognized what was happening in their marriage and sought outside help. For them such speculation was pointless, but for you and your spouse it may prove invaluable. Not only does early detection prevent unhealthy behaviors from becoming lifelong habits, it has the added benefit of avoiding the painful tragedy of infidelity, which is almost always the consequence of ignoring marital difficulties.

ACTION STEPS

- We are often tempted to ignore difficulties in our marriage in order to avoid conflict. This is fine if we are able to accept our differences, but if we resent them, they must be addressed before they become full-blown problems. Now carefully examine your heart to see if there are any hidden resentments or feelings of anger toward your spouse.
- If you do have feelings of resentment or anger, ask the Lord to reveal the source of your feelings. As thoughts and impressions come to you, write them down. Writing often helps to identify clearly what is being felt and why. Once your thoughts are clear, share them with your spouse in a non-accusatory way.

If you cannot resolve these feelings together, then seek outside help—from either a pastor or a Christian counselor. Don't sweep your feelings under the rug. They won't go away unless you resolve the issues that are generating them.

THOUGHT FOR THE DAY

"Maybe it looks like the end to you. After years of trying to keep your marriage together, the pain has just become too acute. How is it possible to forgive when so many wrongs have been done? You're tired of trying and you can't see any way out except divorce, though instead of relief, that option just seems like a route to a different kind of pain. Do you have an ounce left of faith that reconciliation is possible? Consider with us the possibility of the work of putting your marriage back together again. An ounce of faith may be all you need"'[3]

—Jim Talley

SCRIPTURE FOR THE DAY

"The Lord said to me, 'Go, show your love to your wife again, though she is loved by another and is an adulteress. Love her as the Lord loves the Israelites, though they turn to other gods and love the sacred raisin cakes.'"

—HOSEA 3:1

PRAYER

Lord, the pain of infidelity is almost unimaginable. To be betrayed by the one to whom you entrusted the gift of yourself is an unspeakable loss. Give those couples who have known this terrible pain the strength of Your holy love, the strength to forgive, to trust again and to begin anew. Restore their relationship and make their union more than it has ever been, all that You intended marriage to be. In the name of Jesus I pray. Amen.

HONEST CONFESSION AND TRUE REPENTANCE

"No marriage is beyond the reach of God's healing grace. If both partners will make an unconditional commitment to their marriage, and to the Lordship of Jesus Christ, their relationship can be restored. It won't happen instantaneously, and it won't be easy, but it is possible. Healing is a process involving several steps, and it requires both time and commitment.

The first step is often the hardest. It requires both spouses to own their mistakes and to voluntarily make appropriate changes in their personal behavior. In biblical terms this is called confession and repentance. In the case of Dale and Esther (the couple mentioned in the previous chapter), each spouse was required to take responsibility for his/her part in the wounding of their marriage. Initially, each of them was tempted to blame the other.

Esther was inclined to blame Dale for her infidelity: If he had not been so controlling, if he had not been given to angry outbursts, if he had been more sensitive to her needs and desires... The list went on and on. As her pastor/counselor I tried to help her understand that, while Dale's behavior contributed to her unhappiness, he did not cause her to be unfaithful. That was her choice, her way of responding to her pain and unhappiness.

It was even more difficult getting her to understand that her way of reacting to Dale's angry outbursts and controlling manner was also her choice. He did not make her hide her true feelings and opinions. She chose to do that because it was easier than risking a confrontation. It was a natural choice for her, one that she had learned early in her childhood, but a poor one.

For his part, Dale couldn't imagine how Esther could possibly think he was a verbally abusive man. Sure, he got angry from time to time, but that was no big thing—just his way of dealing with stress. Besides, he always apologized. He was a good provider. He was thoughtful, never forgetting her birthday or their wedding anniversary. He was affectionate and helpful. Didn't that count for anything?

To Dale's way of thinking, his good deeds more than made up for his angry outbursts. From Esther's perspective, they were empty acts. "I didn't think he meant them," she explained. "If he really loved me, how could he become so angry at me? How could he scream at me one minute and in the very next breath tell me what a wonderful wife I was? It didn't make sense to me. I couldn't trust my emotions to him. Even if he went days between angry outbursts, I knew it was just a matter of time until it happened again."

When I asked her if she had ever tried to tell Dale how she felt, she said: "I couldn't. Dale's a far better talker than I am, and anytime we argued he always made me feel that it was all my fault. He always made me feel like a bad person, and I hated that feeling."

Thankfully, both Dale and Esther were committed to their marriage and were willing to invest the time and energy necessary to see it restored. Both accepted their part in the terrible tragedy that had befallen them and were willing to do everything in their power to develop healthy ways of relating to each other. The task before them was a difficult one, strewn with many pitfalls, but at least they were ready to begin the rebuilding of their marriage.

ACTION STEPS

- Do you see anything of yourself or your spouse in this account? If so, what? Be specific.
- Examine your own childhood and the way you related to your parents. Was it healthy or unhealthy? In what ways? How has it affected the way you relate to your spouse?
- Are there any changes you need to make in the way you relate to your spouse? If so, decide now how and when you will implement these changes.

THOUGHT FOR THE DAY

"She didn't love me anymore, and that caused her tremendous sadness. She got up and left the bedroom. She went into the living room and sat curled on the sofa, alone and in the dark, and she was dead. And when I came in smelling of sleep and asking what the matter was, she didn't want to see me. Worst of all, the worst thing in the world, my touch repulsed her. My touching her made her cry.

"'I have to hurt you,' she said. The strident voice had turned to whining by now. She wasn't shouting anymore. She was just unspeakably sad. 'I had to hurt you to make you notice me. I hate it. I hate it! And when you do notice me, what do I get? Wally, you are so selfish. At least I know it when I hurt you. You don't even know. I get a red flower in front of the whole congregation. Oh, Wally!'"[1]

—Walter Wangerin, Jr.

SCRIPTURE FOR THE DAY

"Even my close friend, whom I trusted, he who shared my bread, has lifted up his heel against me ... If an enemy were insulting me, I could endure it; if a foe were raising himself against me, I could hide from him. But it is you, a man like myself, my companion, my close friend, with whom I once enjoyed sweet fellowship as we walked with the throng at the house of God."

—PSALM 41:9; 55:12-14

PRAYER

Lord, how could something so beautiful, so good, come to this? How can pain and anger, unfaithfulness and distrust now reign where once there was only love and laughter? Evil is to blame. An ugly act, words spoken angrily, in haste, a tiny hurt carefully kept—these are the things the enemy used to poison the once beautiful relationship. But all is not lost. Where sin does abound, grace does even more abound. What sin has destroyed, You can heal and restore. Come quickly, O Lord, and do Your healing work. In the name of Jesus I pray. Amen.

DEALING WITH YOUR FEELINGS

It is impossible to rebuild a marriage unless the wounded spouse is willing to forgive. As long as he insists on holding her sins against her, there can be no healing for the marriage. Yet, he cannot really forgive until he processes his feelings and comes to closure. If he tries to pronounce forgiveness without working through his feelings, it won't work. His unresolved feelings of hurt and anger will surface time and again to sabotage any attempt to heal the marriage. Yet how does a wounded spouse deal with his anger without destroying the marriage in the process?

As we have seen, there are basically three ways of dealing with anger. The first is the world's way—*express* it. Take revenge, get even. That way has a certain appeal, especially when you've been hurt. But it is terribly destructive. For years Dale dealt with his anger in this manner, and, as a result, he destroyed Esther's love.

The second way is what I call the Church's way—*repress* it. Most Christians deal with their anger by shoving it down. They bury it deep inside themselves. That's the way Esther dealt with hers. Eventually it poisoned her spirit and set her up for an affair.

The third way is God's way—*confess* it. Tell God exactly how you feel. Pour out your hurt and anger to Him. But you can't get stuck here. You've got to release your anger, let go of it. If you don't, confession does nothing but recycle your anger.

When Dale learned of Esther's affair, he was devastated. In an instant his comfortable world was destroyed. At first her confession made no sense. He understood her words, but shock and denial rendered them unreal. This couldn't be happening to him, to them. Not after more than thirty years of marriage. Then the pain hit him, driving him to his knees, reducing his breathing to a strangled wheeze. Finally, he managed a choking whisper, "Why didn't you just take a gun and shoot me? It would have been kinder."

The anger came later, wave after wave of it. And an overwhelming feeling of helplessness. No matter what he did, there was no way to change what had happened. It made no sense to him. How could she do something like this? It went against everything she was, against everything she believed. Grief, greater than anything he had ever experienced, convulsed him. Sobs racked his body as he wept for hours.

Well do I remember his initial telephone call. "Pastor," he said, his voice choked with pain, "Esther's having an affair." When I asked him what he planned to do, he replied, "I've thought about jumping off a cliff, but I don't suppose that's a very good idea." After a short pause he continued, "I need to talk to you. I need some help to sort all of this out."

In our early one-on-one sessions Dale poured out his grief and anger. In explicit detail he told me what he would like to do to Esther's lover. Though I had never heard this Christian man curse, his language was now punctuated with profanity. Yet, even in his anger, he wanted to save his marriage, he wanted to see his relationship with Esther restored.

Patiently, I helped him move from anger to forgiveness. "Forgiveness is an act of the will," I explained. "You begin by telling God how you really feel, that you don't want to forgive Esther, but that, in obedience to His Word, you are choosing to do it anyway. Give God permission to change your feelings, to replace your hurt and anger with a new love for Esther. Then you must forgive her specifically for each sin she committed against you and your marriage."

"What do you mean?" he asked.

"Well, you might pray something like this: 'God, with Your help, I choose to forgive Esther for lying to me about her relationship with Brad. I choose to let go of my hurt and anger.

"'God, with Your help, I choose to forgive Esther for betraying our wedding vows when she had sex with Brad. I choose to let go of my hatred and disgust.'"

"Dale," I went on to say, "you were not sinned against generally but specifically, therefore you must forgive each sinful act specifically."

Finally, he nodded and, in a voice I had to strain to hear, he began, "God, You know that the very thought of the things Esther did with that man makes me sick. When I look at her, I keep imagining them together. Sometimes I just want to run away, so I never have to see her again, but I can't. I want to forgive her, but I want to get even too. I want to hurt her the way she has hurt me, but I know that's not right. Please God, help me to forgive her."

Taking a deep breath, he prayed, "God, I choose to forgive Esther for having sex with Brad. I choose to forgive her for betraying me and the covenant of our marriage…."

Dale prayed for a long time that afternoon, dealing with one painful incident after another, and when he finally finished I knew their marriage could be healed. Not only was he willing to forgive Esther, but equally important, he was willing to address his destructive outbursts and his unhealthy need to control her.

The healing of their marriage was terribly hard work and often painfully slow. Along the way there were several crises. More than once Dale fell back into his old pattern of intimidation and control, causing Esther to withdraw in angry silence. Still, they were both committed to the healing of their marriage, and as the weeks turned into months they began to discover a depth of love and intimacy they had never known.

ACTION STEPS

- Take a few minutes and remember the ways that you have sinned against God and against those you love. Now remember how fully and freely God has forgiven you.
- Search your heart and see if there is any unforgiveness there. If so, honestly confess your feelings to God in prayer. Now specifically let go of your hurt and forgive those who have sinned against you, especially your spouse.

THOUGHT FOR THE DAY

"Painful experiences must be accepted emotionally as well as rationally. When the shock of an experience evokes more pain than can be accepted and assimilated at the moment of impact, then the emotional processing will follow, sometimes days later. This grieving and regrieving is a way of absorbing the full impact of what has occurred and coming to believe it with the heart as well as the head. When the loss is immense as in the … loss of a relationship or the rejection of love, months and sometimes years of mourning may be required before the loss is accepted emotionally. The heart has a memory too, and it must be allowed to feel its pain fully before releasing its hold on the past.

"…Letting go is necessary if one is to find release from the pain. Letting go allows one to flow forward again with the movement of time, to be present once more with oneself, one's companions, one's universe."[1]

—David Augsburger

SCRIPTURE FOR THE DAY

"'Then the master called the servant in. "You wicked servant," he said, "I canceled all that debt of yours because you begged me to. Shouldn't you have had mercy on your fellow servant just as I had on you?" In anger his master turned him over to the jailers to be tortured, until he should pay back all he owed.

"'This is how my heavenly Father will treat each of you unless you forgive your brother from your heart.'"

—MATTHEW 18:32-35

PRAYER

Lord, we so quickly forget our sinful failures and Your great mercy toward us, while we carefully catalog the failures of those who sin against us. Remind us of Your great mercy that we may be merciful toward others. Baptize us in Your unconditional love that we may find the power to forgive those who have sinned against us. In the name of Jesus I pray. Amen.

REBUILDING TRUST

Nothing is more critical to the healing of a marriage than forgiving and forgetting. Forgiveness is not a feeling. It's a choice, an act of the will. The offended spouse chooses to release her hurt and anger, chooses to release her unfaithful spouse from the prison of his sinful past.

If she could, she would gladly erase the hurtful events from her memory, but that's impossible, so she does the next best thing. She refuses to bring them up; refuses, in fact, even to think about them. What's done is done. The past can't be changed, only forgiven. He has confessed his adultery and repented of his sin, so she chooses to turn her attention toward the future, toward the rebuilding of their marriage. When she is tempted, as she is from time to time, to replay the hurtful scenes over and over in her mind, she takes those tormenting thoughts captive. Deliberately she replaces them with memories of their shared happiness. It's not easy, but with God's help it is possible, and the resulting peace is worth all the effort.

Of equal importance is the rebuilding of trust, for without it marriage is hardly more than physical accommodation. Under the best of conditions, trust is built slowly over an extended period of time. To rebuild it now will require not only time, but a concentrated effort on the part of both partners.

The betrayed spouse must choose to place the affair within the larger context of the entirety of the union. Infidelity is inexcusable, and it cannot be tolerated within marriage. But having said that, let me hasten to add that the betrayed spouse must not define the entire relationship by that one tragic event. The marriage is bigger than this affair. Even as a severe toothache can make a person unaware of how good the rest of his body feels, so a painful tragedy, like an affair, can render him temporarily blind to the positive aspects of his marriage.

If you are suffering from a broken marital relationship, remember the good times you have shared, the special moments in the life of your family. These too are a part of your marriage. The affair is an unspeakable tragedy, but it is only a tiny part of your shared life. In time it will become nothing more than a fading memory, a tragic reminder of our sinful humanity.

Dr. Richard Dobbins, founder and director of Emerge Ministries, says, "When an adulterous relationship has broken that bridge of trust, then building it back again frequently requires a healing period ranging from six months to two years.... [The adulterous spouse] must realize that his infidelity has given his mate just cause to be both jealous and suspicious.... The mate who breaks the trust should volunteer information required for the mate whose trust has been shaken to check up on his whereabouts. Discovering that he is in the place he is supposed to be, doing what he said he would be doing, will help to rebuild that trust."[1]

In the case of Dale and Esther, trust was rebuilt slowly. Although Esther agreed to break off all contact with Brad, and immediately terminated her employment as a good-faith gesture, Dale continued to struggle with distrust. Esther tried to reassure him even as she struggled to rebuild her own trust in the marriage. In order to communicate honestly with Dale, she had to risk sharing her true feelings, even the ones she knew he did not approve of. Yet, to do anything less was to doom their future to the unfulfilling dimensions of their past.

Dale had nearly six weeks of vacation time coming, so they decided to go to a Christian retreat which specialized in assisting couples in crisis. The sessions with both the counselor and the group were helpful, but nothing was more beneficial than the many hours they spent together. They took long walks, basking in the quiet beauty of God's creation. Together, they read books, searching for some understanding of how this experience could have happened to them. They shared the Scriptures and prayed together. And they cried together as God's healing grace released their sorrows and healed their hearts. Slowly, they begin to trust again, and with trust came a restoration of their love for one another.

"For the first time ever I began to see myself through Esther's eyes," Dale mused, "and it was not pretty. I had always thought of myself as a good man, affectionate and helpful. Esther recognized these qualities but, for her, they were dwarfed by my anger. From her perspective, our whole relationship was defined by my anger and my need to control her. She was afraid of me and, as we all know, you cannot long love someone you fear."

"It meant a lot to me," Esther confided, "when Dale finally acknowledged how his anger had terrorized our relationship. For the first time I began to take hope. Maybe our marriage could really be different. Maybe I could learn to love him again."

She paused for a moment, a wistful look on her face. "The first time I heard him pray and ask God to guard his lips, I thought, *What a cop-out.* But as he continued to pray the same prayer day after day, I began to notice a change. The angry Dale was gone, and in his place was a kinder, gentler man."

When I raised my eyebrows skeptically, she hastened to add: "He's not perfect yet, but God is really doing a work in his life."

ACTION STEPS

- On a scale of one to ten, with ten being the highest, rate the level of trust in your marriage. Compare your rating with that of your spouse. Discuss any discrepancies there may be in the way you perceive the level of trust in your relationship and the way your spouse perceives it.
- Identify at least three specific ways you can improve trust in your marriage.

THOUGHT FOR THE DAY

"Affairs are never right and never a good way to build a better marriage. But as good can come out of evil, so benefits can come from affairs, even though there are less painful and less sinful ways to accomplish these same purposes."[2]

—Henry A. Virkler

SCRIPTURE FOR THE DAY

"Though you have made me see troubles, many and bitter, you will restore my life again; from the depths of the earth you will again bring me up. You will increase my honor and comfort me once again."

—Psalm 71:20,21

PRAYER

Lord, thank You for being with us in the hour of our unspeakable loss. When it seemed there was nowhere to turn, no one to lean on, You were there. When the pain of personal failure made the future unbearable, You comforted us with Your love. When the pain of betrayal made it nearly impossible to trust again, You gave us hope. Now give us the courage to trust again, that our marriage may be fully restored. In the name of Jesus I pray. Amen.

RESTORING LOST LOVE

Infidelity is an unspeakable tragedy, a deadly wound, but it can also signal a new beginning for the marriage, a rebirth. When an adulterous affair becomes known, it sounds the death knell for the marriage. In some instances, the couple divorces, and the marriage is officially buried. In other cases, they may continue to live together, even though they have no relationship. Their marriage is dead, but not buried. And in some cases, when the old flawed marriage dies, a new, healthier marriage is born. This is what happened in the case of Dale and Esther.

Before they could have a true marriage, though, their old marriage had to die; it was flawed and unhealthy. Their old patterns of relating to each other, the way they communicated, even how they loved, were all tragically impaired. Esther's adultery made all of this painfully obvious, but instead of destroying them, it created a crisis which gave birth to a new beginning for both of them. As they opened their lives, and their marriage, to the work of the Holy Spirit, God began to transform their relationship.

Dale learned to love Esther in a new way. Previously, his love was suffocating. Well do I remember the day he finally realized this fact. "Esther was dying," he said, "not because I didn't love her, but because I loved her too much. She tried to tell me that I was smothering her, but I never understood what she meant."

Tears filled his eyes, and when he spoke again emotion made his voice thick. "A couple of nights ago we watched *Of Mice and Men.* Are you familiar with it?"

Nodding, I replied, "I read the novel years ago. It's by Steinbeck, I think."

"Then you know it's the story of two friends—George and Lennie—or maybe they were cousins. Lennie is simple, probably mentally retarded. A huge giant of a guy who doesn't know his own strength. George tries to look out for him, but

Lennie is always messing things up. He's not mean; in fact, he seems to be tender-hearted in a simple sort of way. Unfortunately, he kills everything he loves—little rabbits, puppies and ultimately the boss's wife. He doesn't mean to kill them, but not knowing his own strength, he squeezes them too tight. And even after they are dead, he goes right on petting them."

"Dale," I asked, "what are you telling me?"

Silent tears ran down his cheeks. "I'm like Lennie," he said, and his voice was fearfully sad. "I squeeze too tight. That's what I did to Esther—I loved her to death. And even when she died, I never noticed. I just went on petting her."

Dale's pain was so obvious I wanted to take him in my arms and comfort him, but before I could, Esther reached over and took his hand. They looked at each with tear-damp eyes. Finally, she said, "We're going to make it."

I couldn't help marveling at how far they had come. They hardly seemed like the same couple. The pain was still there, and it would be for a long time, but there was love there too, and hope. As Esther said, they were going to make it.

Frequently, I am asked, 'Will I ever be able to love my wife again?" or, "After all that we've been through, will I ever be able to love my husband again?" The answer is yes! But it won't happen overnight, and it won't necessarily be easy. When love is restored, however, it will be especially true, for it will be a love born of adversity.

ACTION STEPS

- Examine the way you love your spouse. Is your love liberating or controlling? Is it gentle or demanding? Is it affirming or critical?
- Read I Corinthians 13:4-7. Now compare your love with the love described in these verses.
- Identify two or three specific ways to make your love for your spouse more like the scriptural model in I Corinthians 13.

THOUGHT FOR THE DAY

"Feelings of love usually wither and dry up in a sterile, dry environment. Love needs to be nurtured and fed. And when loving behaviors start to take place without pressure, the feelings of love are often rekindled.... The feelings of love can come back if they are nurtured by the behaviors of love."[1]

—Dr. David Stoop and Jan Stoop

SCRIPTURE FOR THE DAY

"If I speak in the tongues of men and of angels, but have not love, I am only a resounding gong or a clanging cymbal. If I have the gift of prophecy and can fathom all mysteries and all knowledge, and if I have a faith that can move mountains, but have not love, I am nothing. If I give all I possess to the poor and surrender my body to the flames, but have not love, I gain nothing ...

"Love never fails. But where there are prophecies, they will cease; where there are tongues, they will be stilled; where there is knowledge, it will pass away ...

"And now these three remain: faith, hope and love. But the greatest of these is love."

—I CORINTHIANS 13:1-3,8,13

PRAYER

Lord, thank You for the miracle You worked in Dale and Esther's marriage. May it now serve as encouragement for couples who are struggling to save their own marriage. Forgive our sinful failures. Heal our wounded souls. Restore lost love and renew our marriages. In the name of Jesus I pray. Amen.

NINE

Ten Commandments for a Healthy Marriage

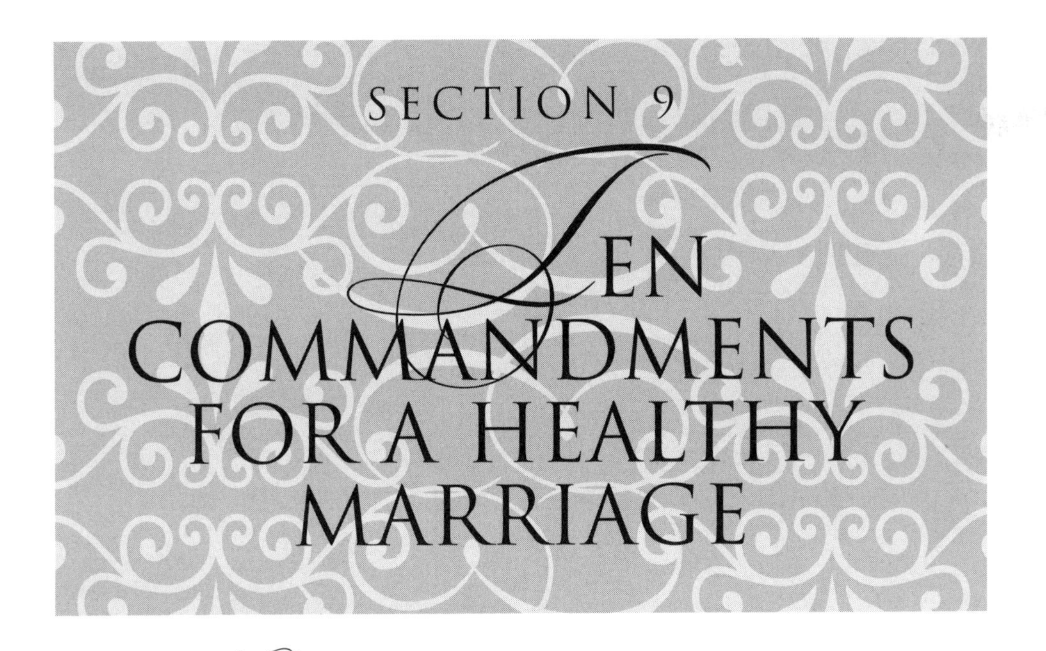

SECTION 9
TEN COMMANDMENTS FOR A HEALTHY MARRIAGE

"Marriage is what you make it. Under God, it must be the most important single thing, in all your life. If your marriage is good, you can overcome anything—financial adversity, illness, rejection, anything. If it is not good, there is not enough success in the world to fill the awful void. Remember, nothing, absolutely nothing, is more important than your marriage, so work at it with love and thoughtfulness all the days of your life.

"Guard it against all intruders. Remember your vows: You have promised, before God and your families, to forsake all others and cleave only to each other. Marriage is made of time, so schedule time together. Spend it wisely in deep sharing. Tell him, tell her, your whole heart. Spend it wisely in fun—laugh and play. Do things together, go places. Spend it wisely in worship—pray together. Spend it wisely in touching—hold each other.

"Remember, a song isn't a song until you sing it. And a bell isn't a bell until you ring it. And love isn't love until you give it away, so give all of your love to each other, all the days of your life."[1]

—Richard Exley

MAKING TIME FOR EACH OTHER[2]

As we have already noted, there is no marriage beyond the reach of God's healing grace. If both partners will commit themselves to each other, and the lordship of Jesus Christ, God can heal their marriage no matter how wounded it is. Yet, how much better to make that kind of commitment before the marriage is wounded by bitterness or infidelity. As the old adage says, "An ounce of prevention is better than a pound of cure."

To affair-proof your marriage, you must give it priority time and energy. You and your mate must spend time together, often and regularly. You must share deeply, fight fairly and forgive freely. Now, that's simple enough, but it's not easy by any means. To love like that demands a lifelong commitment renewed day by day.

On a more specific note, let me share some guidelines that have served Brenda and me well these past forty-one years. We call them the Ten Commandments for a Healthy Marriage.

Commandment #1. Protect your day off at all costs and spend it together, as a couple, and as a family. If an emergency makes it impossible for us to have our regularly scheduled time together, we reschedule another day immediately. Nothing is more important than the time we share!

As a minister and a writer, I have some flexibility to set my own schedule, including my day off. After experimenting with several days, Brenda and I have settled on Monday. There's nothing sacred about Monday, but after Sunday's exhausting schedule we need a day to recover. Besides, there seems to be less scheduled early in the week, making it easier to honor our commitment.

Frequently, we stay in all day, enjoying our privacy and our home. When we do venture out, it is usually just to share a quiet lunch in a nearby restaurant. We talk at length, sharing deeply, catching up on the things we've been too busy to share with each other during the week. We read, listen to music or even watch an old movie.

As a husband, I can tell you that men are not always as sensitive to the need for family time as we should be. When push comes to shove, in the time crunch between family and career, we often end up neglecting our marriage. If this continues for any length of time, resentments begin to build. Faced with an overcommitted husband, one wife I know decided to be creative rather than resentful.

Paula's husband was the pastor of a large congregation, and the demands of ministry were continually encroaching on their family time. In desperation she conspired with his secretary to reschedule all of his appointments for Wednesday afternoon, all day Thursday and Friday. Just before it was time for school to let out, she stopped by the church to see her husband. Sweetly she asked, "Will you please come with me to pick up the children from school?"

"I would like to," Bo replied, "but I have an appointment in ten minutes."

"It's been rescheduled. I checked with your secretary on the way in."

"Well, in that case, let's go."

Once they had picked up all the children, Paula said, "Let's do something really wild and crazy."

Giving her a sharp glance, Bo asked, "Like what?"

"Instead of going back to the church, let's drive to the coast and stay in a condo for two or three days. The kids can play on the beach, and we can spend some quality time together."

Always the practical man, Bo replied. "That's a terrific idea, but this is not a good time. My calendar is really full for the next few days, and we have services tonight, remember. I'm scheduled to preach in about three hours. Besides, by the time we went home and packed our things, it would be after dark before we could get to the coast."

By now the kids were part of the conversation and clamoring to go. "Please, Daddy," they begged. "Let's do it."

They were in Paula's car, and she was driving. Instead of returning to the church, she turned on the highway and headed for the coast. "Be serious, sweetheart," Bo coaxed. "I can't just skip out on the church anytime I want to."

With a mischievous look, Paula said, "Everything is taken care of. Your associate will preach tonight, and your secretary has rescheduled all of your appointments. And I've reserved our favorite condo for the next three nights."

Meekly, he asked, "What about clothes and toiletries? I suppose you've taken care of that too."

"Everything's in the trunk. All you have to do is sit back and relax."

Needless to say, that getaway became the highlight of their year. The children still talk about the time they kidnapped Dad and had him all to themselves for three full days.

Most couples probably don't have that kind of flexibility, but even the most confining schedule and budget can be made to accommodate some creativity. Sometimes all your busy spouse needs is someone who will take charge and plan some real time together. The next time you are tempted to complain that you never have any time together, do something creative instead.

ACTION STEPS

- Examine your calendar for the last ninety days. Have you been giving your family priority on your days off? List some of the things you have done together.
- Ask your spouse if he/she is satisfied with the way you are spending your days off. If he/she is not satisfied, discuss positive ways to improve your family time.

THOUGHT FOR THE DAY

"We also started the tradition of going off alone together. We began to realize we needed extended times alone together—more than just a morning. So we began to look for opportunities to plan just-for-two getaways. We couldn't afford to hire a sitter to come and stay with our children for an extended time, and our parents lived too far away. But we did have friends—very good friends—who offered to keep our three Indians. We reciprocated by keeping their two girls, and we're sure we got the better deal!"[3]

—Dave and Claudia Arp

SCRIPTURE FOR THE DAY

"If a man has recently married, he must not be sent to war or have any other duty laid on him. For one year he is to be free to stay at home and bring happiness to the wife he has married."

—DEUTERONOMY 24:5

PRAYER

Lord, it is so easy to take each other for granted when we live together. I see him/her every day, we eat at the same table and sleep in the same bed. Yet, I am discovering that we are often together without really being together. Genuine togetherness takes planning and effort, it doesn't just happen. Forgive me for MY busyness and preoccupation with my personal responsibilities and interests. Reestablish my priorities. Help me to truly connect with my beloved. In Jesus' name l pray. Amen.

CELEBRATING THE ORDINARY

While preaching on marriage one Sunday morning, I told my congregation that Brenda and I had a special song, "our" song, as it were. "Why," I said, "just thinking about it now, I can almost hear it."

I had cued the sound man ahead of time, and at that very moment he rolled the tape. You can imagine the startled looks I got from my congregation as the melodious voice of John Denver floated through the sanctuary. Then they settled in to eavesdrop on "our" song.

When the song was finished, I asked them to remember the lyrics, the things Denver had sung about. They were ordinary things, every one—supper on the stove, a storm across the valley, the sound of a truck out on the four-lane, the passing of time—hardly the stuff of love songs.

Yet, in another sense, in the truest sense, it was. For a marriage cannot be built only on special times. They are too few. By their very nature, they are rare. That's what makes them special.

Marriage and family have to be made out of sturdier stock, common stuff, made somehow special by the love of those who share it. That's what the next three commandments focus on—ordinary things—eating dinner together, going to bed at the same time and making love. Let's consider them one at a time.

Commandment #2: Eat dinner together. Dinner is a time for sharing and making memories. Don't sacrifice it for lesser things. In our home, Brenda makes even the simplest meal an occasion with candles and soft music. We turn off the television. For that one hour, the world news can wait. If you're addicted to current events, then tape them for later viewing. Don't ruin a lovely dinner by allowing the world to intrude on your shared privacy.

Keep the conversation light and entertaining. Issues can be dealt with at another time. Table talk is for nurturing the relationship, for building family tradition, for renewing the heart of your marriage.

Commandment #3: Go to bed together. Nothing undermines intimacy faster than separate bedtimes. This too is a time for sharing and tenderness. It's an opportunity to touch base with each other, to make sure you haven't let your hectic schedules cause you to drift apart. Without such "set times" for togetherness, you may lose contact with each other in the "busyness" of life.

Commandment #4: Never let anything rob your marriage of the sexual joy God intended. The chances are that one of you is a morning person and the other is a night owl. The resulting differences in your nocturnal habits can put a strain on your love life. Be creative. Nothing says you have to make love at night, after you have given your best energies to other things.

Often it seems that life itself conspires to undermine sexual intimacy. Hectic schedules, a stressful career, financial pressure and the arrival of children all combine to tempt you to make lovemaking a low priority. Resist that temptation or your marriage will be the poorer for it.

Remember, sexual intimacy is a vital part of a healthy marriage. It is a gift from God to be received with thanksgiving and celebrated without shame. It is intended to express love, provide pleasure, cultivate intimacy and propagate the race.

ACTION STEPS

- Are you practicing these four commandments in your marriage? If not, please explain why.
- Spend a few minutes with your spouse discussing these four commandments. Explore ways to integrate them more fully into your own marriage.

THOUGHT FOR THE DAY

"Early Mosaic law made it clear that the emotional well-being of a wife is the specific responsibility of her husband. It was his job to 'cheer' her. Friends and neighbors, it still is! This message is for the man whose own ego needs have drawn him to achieve super success in life, working seven days a week and consuming himself in a continual quest for power and status. If his wife and children do not fit into his schedule somewhere, he deserves the conflict that is certainly coming. This masculine charge should also be heeded by the husband who hoards his nonworking hours for his own pleasures, fishing every weekend, burying his head in the television set, or living on a golf course. Everyone needs recreation and these activities have an important reconstructive role to play. But when our enjoyment begins to suffocate those who need us—those whose very existence depends on our commitment—it has gone too far and requires regulation."[1]

—Dr. James Dobson

SCRIPTURE FOR THE DAY

"He who listens to a life-giving rebuke will be at home among the wise.
He who ignores discipline despises himself, but whoever heeds correction gains understanding.
The fear of the Lord teaches a man wisdom, and humility comes before honor."

—PROVERBS 15:31-33

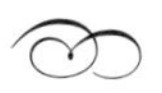

PRAYER

Lord, I have often been too busy, starting out early in the morning and finishing up late at night. With a single-minded obsession, I have pursued my career and interests at the expense of my spouse and children, hardly seeing what I was doing to our family. Forgive my self-centeredness and my insensitivity. Heal the emotional wounds I have inflicted on those I love. Give me another chance, and with Your help I will do better. In the name of Jesus I pray. Amen.

MARITAL PLAY

Your marriage will never be all that God intends until you and your spouse learn to have fun together, which brings us to the fifth commandment for a healthy marriage.

Commandment #5: Play Together. According to K.C. Cole, play is an integral part of all healthy marriages. He writes:

"All happy couples aren't alike, so there is no single litmus test for a good marriage. But if one studies couples systematically over time, it becomes apparent that many of them share a characteristic that signals, more often than not, a healthy union.

"It's nothing so obvious as a satisfying sexual relationship, or shared interests, or the habit of talking out disputes freely. It is, rather, a capacity for playfulness of a kind that transcends fun and reflects considerably more than the partners' ability to amuse each other. Private nicknames, shared jokes and fantasies, mock insults, make-believe fighting—all this might seem like mere silliness. In fact, they may stand in for, or lubricate, more complex transactions, essential but potentially painful or even destructive."[1]

According to R. William Betcher, a Massachusetts clinical psychologist who has studied marital play for several years, "…the common factor in intimate play of all kinds is its ability to stabilize a relationship; it seems to help couples keep a balance between too much distance, which of course alienates them from each other, and too much intimacy, which is apt to be threatening.

"Besides this general function … (play) fills very specific needs. It can serve as an end run around sensitive spots; it can be a way of saying potentially hurtful things voicing criticism, for instance, or expressing wishes that could destroy a marriage if they were actually realized—without hurting anyone. Play is thus a means of defusing conflict. It is also one of the best ways to probe someone's intimate thoughts and feelings, and therefore serves to draw partners together and to cement the bonds between them."[2]

Spontaneous marital play can also enhance intimacy. A scene from the novel *Michael* by G. Robert James is a good example. It is early evening. Michael, a writer, has just finished his day's work when Patricia, his wife, enters with two steaming mugs of spiced tea. Seated in front of a window, which opens on a mountain meadow, they share the tea and the quietness as evening introduces the night. After a bit, Michael plants a kiss on the end of her nose and asks, "...Have I told you today how pretty you are?"

"Oh, Michael, you're silly!" she responds, her pleasure obvious. "I'm seven-and-a-half months pregnant and huge. I can't even walk anymore, I just sort of waddle."

"Well," he said appraising her critically, "now that you mention it your figure does seem a little lumpy."

"You're nothing but a dirty old man," she accuses him feigning anger. "I'm heavy with your child and now you don't want anything more to do with me."

"That's where you're wrong, ma'am," he teased, giving her a lecherous look. "I'm fiendishly interested in women who are seven-and-a-half months pregnant and waddle."

"You fool," she said affectionately as she hoisted herself out of the chair and moved toward the door. "I'll prepare dinner."[3]

Given that kind of tender play, it's not hard to imagine a couple capable of sharing intimacy on all levels—spiritually, emotionally and sexually. Besides, it must be fun to share those witticisms and act out those roles. Lest you think such behavior not fitting for the people of God, let me remind you of Isaac and Rebekah's behavior described in the *King James Version* of Genesis 26:8:

"And it came to pass, when he had been there a long time, that Abimelech king of the Philistines looked out a window, and saw, and, behold, Isaac was sporting with Rebekah his wife."

The Hebrew word for "sporting" literally means to laugh out loud, to play or make sport. Given the context, we can only conclude that Isaac was flirting with Rebekah, participating in some form of love play with her.

Commandment #6: Don't take separate vacations.

There may be rare instances when a separate vacation is unavoidable or even in order, but in general it is not a wise practice. Shared experiences bond couples together, while unshared experiences tend to distance them from one another. Shared vacations often provide the time and relaxation needed to renew a marriage.

Over the years, Brenda and I have been privileged to share several special vacations. There's the trip we took with our daughter when she was thirteen. We visited Carlsbad Caverns, the Grand Canyon, Lake Tahoe, Yosemite National Park, Chinatown and the Golden Gate Bridge in San Francisco, and Disneyland. It was an unforgettable experience, and we talk about it to this day.

Then there's the vacation that we shared with our friends John and Ruth Merrill. At the time they were missionaries living in Brussels, Belgium. Together we took a car tour of Europe. I couldn't possibly begin to recount all of the memorable places we visited, but let me share two or three. The first night we stayed in a bed and breakfast in Holland called the Cheese Farm. It was a working farm, and after a tasty breakfast at the family table, we toured the farm and watched them make cheese. From there we went to the clock shop where Corrie ten Boom and her family hid Jewish people in defiance of the Nazis during World War II. It was a deeply moving experience to stand where they stood and sense something of their courage and their faith.

In Austria we spent the night in a chalet located high in the Alps. As fate would have it, the inn was owned and operated by a former American soldier who had married an Austrian girl. His name was also John Merrill! When we discovered this remarkable coincidence, John and John decided they needed a picture together. I was happy to oblige, and they were soon posed beside our table. A slightly drunk patron decided he wanted in on the fun and demanded that I take his picture also. To appease him I focused the camera and then discharged the flash without releasing the camera shutter. Instantly he became upset. Pointing his finger at me, he kept repeating, "Flash, but no photo. Flash, but no photo." Finally, the proprietor was forced to lead him away in order to avoid an unpleasant scene. For days afterwards we went into spasms of laughter every time one of us would say, "Flash, but no photo."

Later that night we sat on the balcony overlooking the valley below. We talked quietly of the things near to our hearts and drank rich European coffee. Occasionally, the silence of the night was shattered by the bugling of a stag.

Had either Brenda or I taken that vacation alone, it would be impossible to truly share those memorable experiences. And if we tried to force it, in hopes of helping our spouse sense something of the wonder we experienced, we would only create resentment.

Thankfully, we don't take separate vacations, so our special moments are truly shared experiences. Later, such good times can be relived with one another again and again through photographs, slides and videos. With a bit of planning, each shared vacation can become a "second honeymoon." There's no better way to build or enrich your marriage while creating memories that will endure for a lifetime.

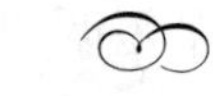

ACTION STEPS

- Examine yourself. Are you fun to live with? Does your partner look forward to being with you? Do you love your mate and family enough to plan fun things to do together?
- Fun can't be forced, but it can be cultivated. With your spouse make a list of fun things that you would like to do together. Your list should include such simple things as going to the carnival or taking in a movie, as well as planning your dream vacation.
- Make specific plans to realize your dream vacation. In the meanwhile, schedule regular times when you do fun things together.

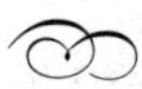

THOUGHT FOR THE DAY

"Tonight was fun 'n' games night around the supper table in our house. It was wild. First of all, one of the kids snickered during the prayer (which isn't that unusual) and that tipped the first domino. Then a humorous incident from school was shared and the event (as well as how it was told) triggered havoc around the table. That was the beginning of twenty to thirty minutes of the loudest, silliest, most enjoyable laughter you can imagine. At one point I watched my oldest literally fall off his chair in hysterics, my youngest doubled over in his chair as his face wound up in his plate with corn chips stuck to his cheeks ... and my two girls leaning back, lost and preoccupied in the most beautiful and beneficial therapy God ever granted humanity: laughter.

"All is quiet now, a rather unusual phenomenon around here. It's almost midnight and although my bones are weary, I'm filled and thrilled with the most pleasant memories a father can enjoy—a healthy, happy, laughing family. What a treasure! The load that often weighs heavily upon my shoulders about this time each week seems light and insignificant now. Laughter, the needed friend, has paid another dividend."[4]

—Charles Swindoll

SCRIPTURE FOR THE DAY

"A cheerful heart is good medicine,
but a crushed spirit dries up the bones."

—PROVERBS 17:22

PRAYER

Lord, I tend to be too serious and, as a consequence, I'm not very much fun to be with. Over the years my seriousness has taken its toll on our marriage. Where once there was fun and laughter, there is now only a wearying somberness. Forgive me, O Lord, for taking myself far too seriously and, in the process, depriving my beloved of the joy which is rightfully his/hers. Restore unto me the joy of Your salvation. Teach me to laugh again that I may truly love. In the name of Jesus I pray. Amen.

DON'T HOLD A GRUDGE

As you probably already know, marriage is a demanding venture. During courtship you saw your spouse on his best behavior. He was dashing and romantic, easy to love. Now you see him, not only at his best, but also at his worst, and he is not always so easy to love. When he leaves his toiletries all over the bathroom counter, after you have asked him not to at least a hundred times, you are tempted to strangle him while he sleeps. When he forgets your birthday, you die a little. When he's late for dinner and doesn't call, you do a slow bum. When he embarrasses you in front of friends, you wonder at his cruelty. After a while all of your feelings merge into one big hurt.

The same is true for him. He hurts too and struggles to understand what happened to the caring lady he married. She doted on him, anticipated his every need, served him before he could ask. Now he's on his own for the most part. When you tell him to make his own sandwich, he wonders why you don't love him anymore. When you go shopping with a friend without telling him, he feels as if he is no longer important to you. And when you refuse his amorous advances two nights in a row, he feels rejected and wonders about his sex appeal. After a while all of those feelings become one—resentment.

What am I trying to say? Simply this: There is enough disappointment in the best marriage to create conflict. Nurse those hurts, focus on them, and it won't be long until you are convinced that your marriage is hopeless. By the same token, there is enough joy, enough love, in that same marriage to warm the coldest heart. Focus on that, and you will be sure that your marriage is a gift from God. Often the only difference between a miserable marriage and a fulfilling one is attitude.

Make up your mind right now that you will not let past hurts rob you of present joy. Remember, if you insist on nursing yesterday's hurts, you will become a prematurely old and bitter person, forfeiting any chance you may have of enjoying the present. Which brings us to the next commandment for a healthy marriage.

Commandment #7: Don't hold a grudge. We have all been hurt by our spouse, by the very one we love the most. That's not the way we would like for it to be, but it is the nature of life on this fallen planet. Once you have been hurt, you have a choice. You can hang on to your hurts and grow bitter, or you can forgive your beloved and get on with the business of living. If you hang on to your hurt, you are saying that it is more important than your marriage.

I once counseled with a man who had been betrayed by his wife. He was deeply wounded and desperately angry. And who could blame him? His wife was having an affair with his best friend. When everything became known, his wife terminated her affair and sought to reconcile with him. In a beautiful demonstration of Christlike grace, he fully forgave her and showered her with his love.

One day we were together so I asked him how he was able to be so forgiving. "This whole experience has taught me many things," he explained. "Initially, I had to decide if I wanted to be part of the problem or part of the solution. I could punish my wife, make her pay for her adultery, but not without punishing myself. I know it doesn't sound very noble, but I just didn't want to suffer anymore. I wanted to put the past behind us and rebuild our life."

He paused and reflected for a moment before continuing. "Once I made that decision, I discovered that forgiving wasn't all that difficult. I found that I could forgive in direct proportion to how much I loved. Since I truly loved my wife, it was natural to forgive her."

Well, forgiveness may have been natural for him, but it is not natural for most of us. And the longer we delay, the longer we harbor our hurt, the harder it becomes to forgive. That's why the Apostle Paul counsels us not to let the sun go down while we are still angry. If we do, he says, we will give the devil a foothold in our lives.[1]

If you can't forgive your spouse simply because you love him/her, do it because you don't want to give the enemy a foothold in your life, or in your marriage. Every unresolved conflict, every unhealed hurt, becomes a seed of bitterness. In its infancy, it is as tiny and as fragile as any other seed. You can blow it away with the breath of forgiveness. But once it takes root in your life, it becomes a tree, and like a tree it is very difficult to uproot.

In my work with hurting couples, I have discovered that virtually every marriage-threatening issue can be traced back to a tiny hurt. Over a period of time it becomes a root of bitterness, and eventually it eats the heart out of the marriage. Most marital tragedy could be avoided if only the wounded spouse would heed Paul's exhortation and release his or her hurt and anger before the day is done.

ACTION STEPS

- Take an emotional inventory of your marriage right now. Are there any unresolved issues, any old hurts, that need to be forgiven and released?
- Once you have identified an old hurt, release it by an act of your will and forgive your spouse. In prayer, give God permission to change your feelings.
- Determine, together with your spouse, that you will not go to bed angry. Make it a point always to resolve your differences before retiring for the night,

THOUGHT FOR THE DAY

"Don't permit the possibility of divorce to enter your thinking. Even in moments of great conflict and discouragement, divorce is no solution. It merely substitutes a new set of miseries for the ones left behind. Guard your relationship against erosion as though you were defending your very lives. Yes, you can make it together. Not only can you survive, but you can keep your love alive if you give it priority in your system of values."[2]

—Dr. James Dobson

SCRIPTURE FOR THE DAY

"'So do not fear, for I am with you; do not be dismayed, for I am your God. I will strengthen you and help you; I will uphold you with my righteous right hand.

All who rage against you will surely be ashamed and disgraced; those who oppose you will be as nothing and perish.

Though you search for your enemies, you will not find them.

Those who wage war against you will be as nothing at all.

For I am the Lord, your God, who takes hold of your right hand and says to you, Do not fear; I will help you."

—ISAIAH 41:10-13

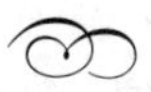

PRAYER

Lord, search my heart and my life. Root out any hurt, any bitterness, any unforgiveness. Give me a forgiving spirit and a heart of love. Give me eyes to see, not the hurts and disappointments, but the joys of my marriage. O Lord, I make a covenant with You right now—by Your grace I will not let the sun go down on my wrath. In the name of Jesus I pray. Amen.

BUILD A SPIRITUAL FOUNDATION

In order for your marriage to be all that it can be, it must have a spiritual foundation. Initially, you and your mate may have been attracted to each other for physical or romantic reasons, but if your marriage is to stand the test of time, it must be made of sturdier stuff. When the inevitable storms of life come, only those marriages that are built on a spiritual foundation will stand. With these thoughts in mind, let's turn our attention to the last three commandments for a healthy marriage.

Commandment #8: Pray together. Nothing is more intimate than your relationship with God. When you invite your spouse to share that experience with you, you are opening the deepest part of your being to him or her. It can be threatening at first, but discipline yourself to pray together. The rewards will more than justify the effort.

Marital prayers should be brief and honest. Brenda and I have found that bedtime works best for us. As we lie side by side, we hold hands and pray sincerely about the true concerns and real joys of our hearts. By so doing, we lift our shared life up to the Lord.

The goal of marital prayer is not personal spiritual development, but marital development. We use this time as an opportunity to present our personal and family needs to God. We seek His counsel and guidance regarding important decisions. We ask His blessing upon our marriage and our children. We surrender to Him daily that He may work His will in and through our lives.

Commandment #9: Little things mean a lot. In fact, they can make the difference between a mediocre marriage and a really good one. It's usually not the expensive gifts or the foreign vacations that determine the quality of a marital relationship, but the little things. A love note in his lunch box or an "unbirthday" card for her. A kind word, help with the children, a listening ear, the feeling that he/she really cares.

Commandment #10: Pledge yourselves, not only to physical faithfulness, but to emotional fidelity as well. Do not allow friends, family or career to meet your "belonging needs." These you must provide for each other. They are the heart and soul of your relationship.

Studies have shown that emotional bonding is the primary cause of infidelity, especially when the persons involved are both Christians. Inappropriate emotional bonding usually occurs in one of two ways. The first way is through need satisfaction. We all have a built-in need for closeness, kindness, tenderness and togetherness. When these needs are not being met in our marriage, we are tempted to find someone with whom we can emotionally connect. Even if nothing sexually inappropriate has transpired, we are nonetheless guilty of emotional adultery when we meet emotional needs for each other, which can legitimately be met only by our spouse. And if immediate steps are not taken to rectify the situation, a full-blown affair is only a matter of time.

The second way inappropriate emotional bonding occurs is through improper confidences. It is always improper to share marital difficulties with a friend of the opposite sex. When a man shares the frustrations and disappointments in his marriage with another woman, he betrays his wife's trust and compromises the emotional fidelity of their marriage. Likewise, when he entertains the confidences of another woman, he again betrays the emotional intimacy he shares with his wife. Of further concern is the fact that the sharing of such personal matters inevitably leads to a need for privacy, the privacy to physical consolation, and physical consolation straight to bed.

Succumbing to sexual sin is seldom sudden. Rather, it is the culmination of a series of small temptations. Therefore, it is critically important that we establish appropriate boundaries before temptation whispers its beguiling suggestions. And no boundary is more important than a mutual pledge to emotional fidelity.

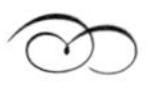

ACTION STEPS

- Review the Ten Commandments for a Healthy Marriage:
  1) Protect your day off and spend it together.
  2) Eat dinner together.
  3) Go to bed together.
  4) Never let anything rob your marriage of the sexual joy God intended.
  5) Play together.
  6) Don't take separate vacations.
  7) Don't hold a grudge.
  8) Pray together.
  9) Little things mean a lot.
  10) Pledge yourselves, not only to physical faithfulness, but to emotional fidelity as well.
- Rate yourself on each of these ten commandments using a scale of one to ten, with ten being the best score. Are you satisfied with your performance? If not, where would you like to improve?
- With your spouse discuss specific ways to integrate these commandments more fully into your daily lives. Take it one step at a time. Don't tackle more than you can handle. Agree together with your spouse on the first step and develop a specific plan for implementing it.

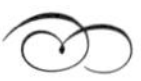

THOUGHT FOR THE DAY

"In reality, marriage is both a gift and a discipline. God gives us each other and the tools for cultivating our blessed oneness, but it is up to us to work the soil of our relationship all the days of our life."[1]

—Richard Exley

SCRIPTURE FOR THE DAY

"My son, pay attention to what I say; listen closely to my words.
Do not let them out of your sight, keep them within your heart; for they are life to those who find them and health to a man's whole body.
Above all else, guard your heart, for it is the wellspring of life.
Put away perversity from your mouth; keep corrupt talk far from your lips.
Let your eyes look straight ahead, fix your gaze directly before you.
Make level paths for your feet and take only ways that are firm.
Do not swerve to the right or the left; keep your foot from evil."

—PROVERBS 4:20-27

PRAYER

Lord, I have to confess that I haven't always lived up to the Ten Commandments for a Healthy Marriage. I work too much and play too little. Sometimes I miss dinner with my family, and my work takes me away from home more than I would like. I have a tendency toward self-pity, and I can harbor a hurt with the best of them. Some nights I'm too tired to pray, and I tend to overlook the little things. And when I'm not connecting emotionally with my beloved, I'm tempted to seek understanding and appreciation wherever I can find it. I guess what I'm trying to say is that without Your help I am in deep trouble. Forgive my failures. Make me the kind of spouse and parent I should be. In the name of Jesus I pray. Amen.

TEN
BUILDING MARRIAGES THAT LAST

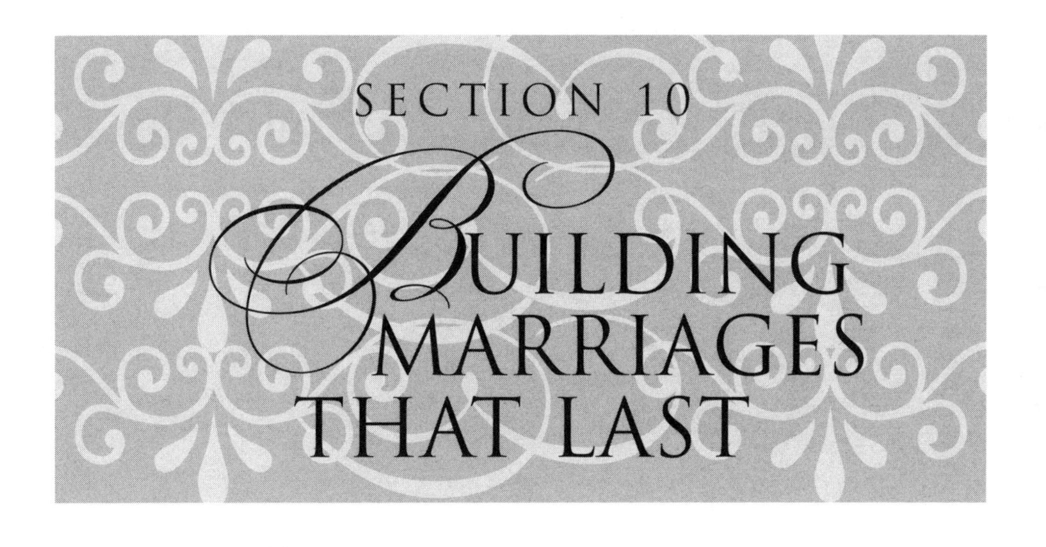

"When the story of your family is finally written, what will the record show? Will you cultivate an intimate marriage, or will you journey relentlessly down the road toward divorce proceedings, with consequent property settlement, custody battles, and broken dreams? How will you beat the odds? Fortunately, you are not merely passive victims in the unfolding drama of your lives together. You can build a stable relationship that will withstand the storms of life. All that is required is the desire to do so … with a little advice and counsel."[1]

—Dr. James C. Dobson

A LOVE STORY[2]

Several years ago Erich Segal wrote *Love Story,* a tenderly funny and poignant story of two young people who fall in love and marry. It became an instant best-seller and was later made into a movie, but it cannot compare with the real-life love story of the late John and Harriet McCormack.

"They were married fifty-two years and never spent a night apart.... Dr. Billy Graham referred to their marriage as one of the great love stories of our generation. He said there was a very deep spiritual affinity between them that was far more binding than the psychological or the physical. Roger Brooks, their chauffeur of twenty years, declared, 'They were just like newlyweds.'

"Harriet McCormack was eighty-seven years old when she died, and age had worked a cruel toll in her declining years. It had narrowed her vision, and forced her to hide her dark eyes behind glasses. Arthritis, stemming from a leg injury, had slowed her walk to infant steps. Even eating had become a chore, the food had to be soft and in small pieces. Once, at a White House State dinner, John McCormack was observed cutting his wife's meat.

"When Harriet was hospitalized in her eighty-seventh year, John took the hospital room next to hers and kept the door open between them at all times so he could hear her if she called during the night. When she was too warm he bathed her forehead. When she was weak he fed her. When she could no longer eat solid foods, he did not; if she had to endure roast mush, he would endure it with her. In the small hours of the morning her soft moan would come, 'John, John, where are you?' and he would scuffle into his slippers and tug on his bathrobe. 'I'm right here, Harriet, don't worry.' When she slipped into the past, he was not impatient. He went with her. 'I'm so glad I can help her there.' he told John Monohan, 'I can remember her brothers and sisters.'

"He sat there day after day, hour after hour, according to Jo Meegan, and would repeat everything. He would recall all their early life together with great fondness.... When people talked about sacrifice, he scoffed at them. What did they mean? He wanted to be with Harriet. He was annoyed when anyone suggested duty. Duty wasn't love."[3]

Now, I believe with all my heart that this is what God had in mind when He said, "...'It is not good for the man to be alone. I will make a helper suitable for him."[4] Yet how few marriages ever approach this divine ideal. Studies indicate that only about 10 percent of all marriages reach their relational potential, the rest struggle along in mediocrity or end in divorce.

Yet, it is not blind fate that separates the John and Harriet McCormacks from those whose marriages fail to reach their relational potential. The difference is desire and commitment. Any couple can have a great marriage if they are willing to invest the time and effort. The truly great marriages have at least five characteristics in common—personal wholeness, a genuine commitment to the marriage, deep sharing, a willingness to own one's mistakes and a willingness to forgive. Cultivate these traits, and you can build a marriage that will last!

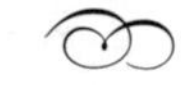

ACTION STEPS

- Spend a few minutes identifying some of the more obvious characteristics that made John and Harriet McCormack's marriage so special. Are these same traits active in your marriage?
- Identify three or four other couples who have a good marriage and see if you can identify the traits that set their marriages apart.
- Rate your marriage:

  _____ in trouble

  _____ poor

  _____ fair

  _____ good

_____ very good

_____ excellent

- Compare the way you rated your marriage with the way your spouse rated it. Discuss the reasons each of you rated the marriage the way you did. Agree on specific ways you can work together to improve your relationship.

THOUGHT FOR THE DAY

"Because marriage is potentially the most totally intimate of human relationships, it is both the most difficult relationship, on the one hand, and the most rewarding, on the other. It is the place where most adults have the opportunity to lessen their loneliness, satisfy their heart-hungers, and participate in the wonderfully creative process of self-other fulfillment."[5]

—Howard and Charlotte Clinebell

SCRIPTURE FOR THE DAY

"Wives, submit to your husbands, as is fitting in the Lord.

"Husbands, love your wives and do not be harsh with them.

"Children, obey your parents in everything, for this pleases the Lord.

"Fathers, do not embitter your children, or they will become discouraged."

—COLOSSIANS 3:18-21

PRAYER

Lord, I am deeply moved by the kind of loving commitment John McCormack had for his beloved Harriet. Her physical ailments did not embarrass him, nor did her inability to separate the past from the present. In the hour of her need, he was neither condescending nor impatient. I am not so naive as to believe that his tender kindness came naturally. Rather, I think, it was the fruit of a lifetime of discipline. Teach me to be kind and helpful toward my spouse, now, in the sunshine of our lives, so that I may be prepared to minister loving kindness when the darkness comes. In the name of Jesus I pray. Amen.

PERSONAL WHOLENESS

It is impossible to build a healthy marriage between unhealthy people, or to build a whole marriage between wounded people. In short, a marriage is no better, no stronger, than the two people who marry. As someone once said, "You can't make a good omelet out of bad eggs."

Persons who are unhappy, wounded or bitter, find it almost impossible to build a lasting marriage. Because of their past hurts and disappointments, they continually misinterpret and overreact, thus destroying the very thing they most desire—emotional intimacy.

A common temptation, given this information, is to critically evaluate one's spouse. Perhaps he or she is unwhole. Maybe some past hurt, some unresolved disappointment in his or her life, is now undermining the integrity of the marriage. That may indeed be the case in your marriage, but it should not be your concern. Instead of examining your spouse, let me encourage you to search your own heart and life. In prayer, ask the Lord to reveal any personal woundedness that might compromise the marriage relationship.

"How," you may be wondering, "can I tell if I am harboring some marriage-compromising hurt?" There are basically two clues. The first is found in your relationships. Did you have a troubled childhood? Do you currently have a good relationship with your parents and siblings? Are your current friendships healthy and long-standing, or do you have a history of volatile, short-term relationships? Emotionally healthy people are usually the product of a good childhood, and their current relationships are healthy and long-standing. Unwhole people, on the other hand, usually have a troubled family history and a pattern of volatile, short-term relationships.

The second clue is found in the way you respond to the vicissitudes of life. Is your response commensurate to the event that triggered it, or is it disproportionate? Emotionally healthy people demonstrate appropriate emotional responses, while wounded people tend to overreact or to manifest inappropriate emotions.

Let me illustrate. In the novel, *The Prince of Tides,* Tom Wingo uses humor to deal with both his pain and his anger. Casually he explains his behavior as, "the southern way." But it is not the southern way. It is Tom Wingo's way. When something hurts too much, like his brother's death, or his twin sister's attempted suicide or his childhood memories, he copes by being funny. Humor, however, is an inappropriate, and unhealthy, way of dealing with grief. As a result, Tom grows emotionally distant from those closest to him, including his wife.

His inability to respond to Luke's death with the appropriate emotion is evidence of a far deeper dysfunction. And as the story unfolds, we are given glimpses into his terrifying childhood. A childhood marked by domestic violence, sexual abuse and secrecy. And, as Tom tells his sister's psychiatrist, the secrecy is the worst.

It is no wonder, then, that he cannot be emotionally intimate with his wife. If he lets Sallie get too close to him, she might discover his secrets. Finally, his ambivalence toward her becomes unbearable, and she confronts him. This time she will not be put off by his humor or his self-pity.

"It's hurting us, Tom."

"I know ... To my surprise, I'm not a good husband. I once thought I'd be a great one. Charming, sensitive, loving, and attentive to my wife's every need. I'm sorry, Sallie. I haven't been good for you in such a long time. It's a source of great pain. I want to be better. I'm so cold, so secretive. I swear I'll do better....

"You blame your parents for so much, Tom. When does it start becoming your own responsibility? When do you take your life into your own hands? When do you start accepting the blame or credit for your own actions?"[1]

If, like Tom Wingo, you have discovered that your past, with its hurts and disappointments, has invaded your marriage, let me urge you to stop blaming others and take responsibility for your actions. With the help of a pastor or Christian counselor, you can overcome the past. You can be made whole. Then, and only then, will your marriage be all that you long for it to be.

ACTION STEPS

- Please answer the following questions:

  1) Do I have any unresolved hurts or conflicts from my childhood or adolescence? If you answered yes, please list them.

  2) Do I overreact when my spouse and I have a disagreement? If you answered yes, please examine the source of your reaction. It probably has little or nothing to do with the present situation.

  3) Am I truly transparent with my spouse, or do I have secrets that I cannot share with him/her? Why can't you share your secrets?

- If you answered yes to at least two of the above questions, let me urge you to see your pastor or a Christian counselor. Emotional wholeness is foundational to a healthy marriage, therefore it is imperative that you get the help you need in resolving these issues.

THOUGHT FOR THE DAY

"Perhaps your memories are painful.... Your past seems like a nuclear winter, desolate and frozen. Don't turn away! As painful as it may be, that too is who you are. Deny it, and you deny a part of yourself. Repress it, and you sentence yourself to a lifetime of irrational responses and misdirected outbursts. Embrace it. Feel the pain. Shed the tears you have so long withheld. You are not alone. Jesus is with you, and He will redeem your past (that is, make it contribute to your ultimate Christlikeness)."[2]

—Richard Exley

SCRIPTURE FOR THE DAY

"The lamp of the Lord searches the spirit of a man; it searches out his inmost being."

—PROVERBS 20:27

PRAYER

Lord, no one comes through childhood and adolescence unscathed. We all have our wounds. Unhealed, they cloud our vision, distort reality and undermine the sanctity of our marriage. Today I bring You my wounds. They have imprisoned me far too long. Heal my insecurities and deliver me from the jealousies they have birthed. Redeem my pain, turn it into loving compassion. May even the tragedies of my life become redemptive tools in Your hands. Make me whole, Lord, that I may become the kind of spouse and parent You have called me to be. In Jesus' name l pray. Amen.

THE HIGH COST OF COMMITMENT[1]

In March 1990, Dr. Robertson McQuilkin announced his resignation as president of Columbia Bible College in order to care for his beloved wife, Muriel, who was suffering from the advanced stages of Alzheimer's disease. In his resignation letter he wrote:

"My dear wife, Muriel, has been in failing mental health for about eight years. So far I have been able to carry both her ever-growing needs and my leadership responsibilities at CBC. But recently it has become apparent that Muriel is contented most of the time she is with me and almost none of the time I am away from her. It is not just 'discontent.' She is filled with fear—even terror—that she has lost me and always goes in search of me when I leave home. Then she may be full of anger when she cannot get to me. So it is clear to me that she needs me now, full-time.

"Perhaps it would help you to understand if I shared with you what I shared at the time of the announcement of my resignation in chapel. The decision was made, in a way, forty-two years ago when I promised to care for Muriel 'in sickness and in health...till death do us part.' So, as I told the students and faculty, as a man of my word, integrity has something to do with it. But so does fairness. She has cared for me fully and sacrificially all these years; if I cared for her for the next forty years I would not be out of debt. Duty, however, can be grim and stoic. But there is more; I love Muriel. She is a delight to me—her childlike dependence and confidence in me, her warm love, occasional flashes of that wit I used to relish so, her happy spirit and tough resilience in the face of her continual distressing frustration. I do not have to care for her, I get to! It is a high honor to care for so wonderful a person."[2]

As a man and a husband, I am deeply moved when I read that. Intuitively I realize that's the stuff real marriages are made of—commitment and integrity, for better or for worse. Yet it would be a mistake for us to assume that Dr. McQuilkin's decision was an isolated choice, independent of the hundreds of lesser choices that went into their forty-two years of marriage. In truth, a decision of that magnitude is almost always the culmination of a lifelong series of smaller, daily decisions. And, as such, it challenges every one of us to examine the choices we make each day and the way we relate to our spouse.

ACTION STEPS

- Ask yourself: Does my marriage get the leftovers and scraps from my busy day, or do I give it priority time and energy?
- Make a list of the "little" ways in which you regularly lay down your life for your spouse. Things like giving up Monday night football to spend the evening with her, or giving up a Saturday shopping trip to go fishing with him.
- Based on your daily decisions, do you think you could give up your career in order to care for your spouse if he/she became an invalid?

THOUGHT FOR THE DAY

"... nothing is easier than saying words.

Nothing is harder than living them, day after day.

What you promise today must be renewed and redecided tomorrow and each day that stretches out before you."[3]

—Arthur Gordon

SCRIPTURE FOR THE DAY

"Husbands, love your wives, just as Christ loved the church and gave himself up for her to make her holy, cleansing her by the washing with water through the word, and to present her to himself as a radiant church, without stain or wrinkle or any other blemish, but holy and blameless."

—EPHESIANS 5:25-27

PRAYER

Lord, I would like to think that I would give up my career to care for my beloved, but self-honesty makes me wonder. If I cannot be selfless in the little decisions that make up our marriage, why should I think I would fare any better in the moment of crisis? Teach me to live and love selflessly day by day so that I will be prepared to lay down my life for my spouse should that day ever come. In the name of Jesus I pray. Amen.

DEEP SHARING[1]

In his novel, *Of Mice and Men,* John Steinbeck has a poignant exchange in which a crippled black man laments his loneliness:

"'A guy needs somebody…' Crooks said gently, 'Maybe you can see now. You got George. You know he goin' to come back. S'pose you didn't have nobody. S'pose you couldn't go into the bunkhouse and play rummy 'cause you was black. How'd you like that? S'pose you had to sit out here an' read books. Sure you could play horseshoes till it got dark, but then you got to read books. Books ain't no good. A guy needs somebody—to be near him.' He whined, 'A guy goes nuts if he ain't got nobody. Don't make no difference who the guy is, long's he's with you. I tell ya,' he cried, 'I tell ya, a guy gets too lonely an' he gets sick.'"[2]

And Crooks was right, if a person gets too lonely, he gets sick. But he was sadly mistaken to think that all a person needs is a physical presence. In truth, some of the loneliest people I know are married. For them, loneliness is lying awake in the dead of night tormented by the regular breathing of their sleeping spouse: If only he had time to hear the cry of her heart, to know her secret fears and share her tentative dreams. If only he could tell her of the aching emptiness he feels deep inside. If only they could really connect. Not just physically, but emotionally as well. If only they could be soul mates, sharing their true selves with each other.

What they hunger for is a level of communication that is rare indeed. I call it deep sharing, and it is more than mere talking, more even than what the marriage experts call communication. It is the sharing of your very life. Not just the surface issues either, but the heart and soul of who you truly are—your hidden fears, your secret dreams, the longings too deep for words. Without it, your marriage may be good, but it will never be great.

There are a number of reasons why couples rarely, if ever, experience deep sharing. In order to share on this level, a person must possess an intimate self-knowledge. He must know who he truly is, and must seek to understand how his past experiences have shaped him, and how they continue to influence his perception of present events and relationships. He must be able to accept his innermost feelings as valid before he can allow his spouse to share her deepest feelings with him. If he has not come to terms with his own feelings, any attempt by his spouse to share deeply will be too threatening.

The Scriptures give us several pictures of the personal transparency inherent in this kind of sharing. When Adam and Eve became man and wife, the Bible says, "The man and his wife were both naked, and they felt no shame."[3] In addition to physical nudity, they were emotionally naked; that is, they had nothing to hide from each other, no secrets. And it was this total transparency that enabled them to truly become one flesh. As C. S. Lewis said, "Eros will have naked bodies; friendships [marriage] naked personalities."[4]

We see this picture again in the friendship between David and Jonathan. After they made a covenant of friendship, "Jonathan took off the robe he was wearing and gave it to David, along with his tunic, and even his sword, his bow and his belt."[5]

When Jonathan disrobed, he made himself transparent to David. It was his way of saying that he had nothing to hide, that he wanted David to know the real Jonathan. A friendship, let alone a marriage, built on anything less than this kind of transparency is just a sham—a make-believe relationship between two people who are pretending to be something other than who they really are.

Inherent in this kind of relationship is personal vulnerability. When Jonathan gave David his weapons—his sword, his bow, and his belt—he made himself vulnerable. He was at David's mercy. He had no way to defend himself. So it is in a marriage where there is deep sharing. When we share our deepest self with our spouse, we are giving him/her the knowledge (weapons) with which to destroy us. It is the ultimate act of trust, and it is what distinguishes the truly great marriages from those that are just average.

This kind of deep sharing is only possible in an atmosphere of unconditional acceptance. If one of the spouses is judgmental, the other will soon learn to say "right" things rather than "real" things. It will be safer, less confrontational, but it will not be intimate. To be truly intimate, we must share our deepest selves; it is the only way.

"Personal meaning and human value arise only in relationship. Solitude casts doubt on them. Identity, too, is discovered only in relationship. Lacking companions at the level of the soul, I finally cannot find my soul. It always takes another person to show myself to me. Alone, I die."[6] And I am alone, even within marriage, unless we can share deeply.

ACTION STEPS

- In order to share deeply, you must first be in touch with your deepest feelings, your real self. This doesn't just happen. It requires a deliberate effort. Solitude and introspection are mandatory. Journaling is often a helpful way of clarifying your feelings. Determine now to begin this inward journey in order to share deeply with your spouse.
- Ask your spouse if you are judgmental or accepting toward his/her ideas and feelings, especially if they differ from your own. Listen carefully to his/her response and do not defend yourself regardless of what he/she says. If he/she perceives that you are judgmental, it makes no difference whether you think you are or not, he/she will not share deeply.
- Make a conscious effort to practice unconditional acceptance toward the ideas and feelings expressed by your spouse.

THOUGHT FOR THE DAY

"With the people I know very well, I find that all of the emotion that would normally be expressed in the face is there in the voice: the tiredness, the anxiety, the suppressed excitement. My impressions based on the voice seem to be just as accurate as those of sighted people. The capacity of the voice to reveal the self is truly amazing. Is the voice intelligent? Is it colorful? Is there light and shade? Is there melody, humor, gracefulness, accuracy? Is it gentle, amusing and varied? On the other hand is the voice lazy? Is it flat, drab and monotonous? Is the range of vocabulary poor and used without precision and sensitivity? These are the things that matter to me now."[7]

—John M. Hull, blind at age 48

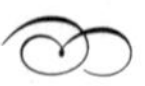

SCRIPTURE FOR THE DAY

"For this very reason, make every effort to add to your faith goodness; and to goodness, knowledge; and to knowledge, self-control; and to self-control, perseverance; and to perseverance, godliness; and to godliness, brotherly kindness; and to brotherly kindness, love. For if you possess these qualities in increasing measure, they will keep you from being ineffective and unproductive in your knowledge of our Lord Jesus Christ."

—2 PETER 1:5-8

PRAYER

Lord, I hunger for deep sharing in our marriage. I long to truly know my beloved and to be known by him/her. Unfortunately, I have a long history of trying to tell him/her what he/she should feel. As a result, he/she now keeps his/her deepest feelings to himself/herself and only shares with me the thoughts and feelings that he/she thinks I will approve of. Forgive my arrogance, Lord. Teach me to accept his/her thoughts and feelings unconditionally. In the name of Jesus I pray. Amen.

THE GIFT OF FORGIVENESS

It is December 24, 1988, and for the first time ever Brenda and I are celebrating Christmas alone. Determining to make the best of it, I build a fire in the fireplace and light the kerosene lamps on the mantle while Brenda prepares eggnog in the kitchen.

After a bit, she comes to join me in front of the fire, but instead of sitting beside me on the love seat, she kneels behind me and puts both arms around my neck. "I have something for you," she says, handing me a red envelope.

A Christmas card, I think, *how nice.* Then I see a handwritten note beneath the printed verse. As I begin to read it, my eyes grow misty, and my throat aches, so great is the lump that forms there.

In an instant, I am transported back to a Sunday afternoon in August nearly ten years earlier. We are quarreling as we have done numerous times before during our thirteen-year marriage. I've long since forgotten what started, some insignificant thing most likely, but it soon turns deadly.

And then Brenda speaks the words that seem to seal my fate. "I hate you," she sobs, "I hate you! Once I loved you with all my heart, but you have killed my love. I can't live this way. I won't. When Leah graduates, I'm going to divorce you."

Stumbling beneath the awful weight of her terrible pain, she flees the room, leaving an unbearable emptiness in her wake. I hear the bathroom door close, then lock. A heavy sadness envelops me. Never have I felt so alone, so helpless.

Descending the stairs toward my study, I fight back my own tears. I try to tell myself that Brenda doesn't really mean what she said. She is just angry. She wouldn't really divorce me. Surely not.

Like a zombie, I go through the motions of preparing a sermon for the evening service. But my mind is grappling with weightier matters. What will I do if Brenda really does leave me when Leah graduates? How will I cope? I truly love her, even if she cannot imagine that I do. And I can change, I will show her.

Yet, even in the aftermath of the revelation of how my anger is destroying her, I am tempted to rationalize, to somehow justify my behavior. I am not a bad man. I compliment Brenda often and express my love to her every day. I am affectionate, appreciative, and I never forget her birthday, or our anniversary. I write her poems and take her out to dinner. Doesn't that count for something?

After a long time I make my way upstairs to dress for church. Leah is at the table eating a sandwich when I pass the dining room, and I pause for a moment in the doorway. Brenda glances my way, but she doesn't say anything. Finally, I ask her if she is ready for church. In a voice that sounds a hundred years old she tells me she isn't going. Nothing more, just that. Sadly, I turn away and continue toward the bedroom. *So this is what it is going to be like,* I remember thinking.

We never speak of that tragic Sunday afternoon again. Never. But for years, nine years and four months to be exact, that painful moment lies like a piece of misplaced furniture in the soul of our marriage. Anytime we try to get close to each other, we bump into it.

As the years pass, things seem to improve between us. Many a night I lie on the bed watching Brenda as she prepares to join me and think how blessed we are. Not infrequently I ask her, "Do you think anyone is as happy as we are?" Giving me a quick smile and a hug, before turning out the light, she says, "I'm sure there are others just as happy."

Lying in the darkness I think, *It's going to be all right. She's happier now, I can tell.* But oh, how I long to hear her say, "Richard, all is forgiven. I don't hate you anymore. I love you." I can't ask though, lest I awaken her old hurts. I can only wait. And hope.

In May 1988 Leah graduates from high school and leaves home to begin a life of her own. Now it is just the two of us. June turns into December, and before we hardly know it, it is Christmas Eve...

Straining to make out Brenda's words through tear-blurred eyes I return to the present. Haltingly, I read: "I Brenda Starr take thee Richard Dean to be my lawfully wedded husband. To have and to hold from this day forward. For richer, for poorer, in sickness and in health, till death do us part. To love, honor, cherish and obey. Forsaking all others and thereto I plight thee my troth. In the name of the Father, the Son and the Holy Ghost.

"It looks like you're stuck with me! I'm not going anywhere! Always remember, 'I'll never leave thee nor forsake thee.'

Your Devoted Wife & Lover,
Brenda Starr"

All at once I am undone, overwhelmed, by such mercy and grace. Turning to Brenda I crush her to my chest. The awful burden of ten long years is lifted. The dark cloud of condemnation is dissipated. That misplaced piece of furniture is gone. There is nothing between us. In the soul of our marriage there is only love, and we are one.

ACTION STEPS

- Our marriage was healed and restored because I was willing to own my mistakes, and Brenda was willing to forgive me. Examine your marriage and see if you have made any mistakes that you have not been willing to own. If there are any, specifically identify them now and honestly confess them to your spouse.
- Now examine your marriage and see if you are harboring any unforgiveness toward your spouse. If so, determine right now that you are going to forgive him/her.

THOUGHT FOR THE DAY

"Dear Lord Jesus, where did this come from, this sudden, unnatural, undeserved willingness to let me touch her, hug her, love her? Not from me! I was her ruination. Not from her, because I had killed that part of her. From You!

"How often had we hugged before? I can't count the times. How good had those hugs been? I couldn't measure the goodness. But this hug—don't you know, it was my salvation, different from any other and more remarkable because this is the hug I should never have had. That is forgiveness! The law was gone. Rights were all abandoned. Mercy took their place. We were married again. And it was You, Christ Jesus, in my arms—within my graceful Thanne. One single, common hug, and we were alive again."[1]

—Walter Wangerin, Jr.

SCRIPTURE FOR THE DAY

"The teachers of the law and the Pharisees brought in a woman caught in adultery. They made her stand before the group and said to Jesus, 'Teacher, this woman was caught in the act of adultery. In the Law Moses commanded us to stone such women. Now what do you say?' They were using this question as a trap, in order to have a basis for accusing him.

"But Jesus bent down and started to write on the ground with his finger. When they kept on questioning him, he straightened up and said to them, 'If any one of you is without sin, let him be the first to throw a stone at her.' Again he stooped down and wrote on the ground.

"At this, those who heard began to go away one at a time, the older ones first, until only Jesus was left, with the woman still standing there. Jesus straightened up and asked her, 'Woman, where are they? Has no one condemned you?'

"'No one, sir,' she said.

"'Then neither do I condemn you,' Jesus declared. 'Go now and leave your life of sin.'"

—JOHN 8:3-11

PRAYER

Lord, I thank You for the unspeakable gift of Your forgiveness. And I thank You for enabling my beloved to forgive me as well. I do not deserve to be forgiven, and yet he/she has forgiven me and restored me to his/her love. I have been given a second chance, a new beginning. With Your help, I will make the most of it. I will love him/her all the days of my life, and together we will build a marriage that lasts. In the name of Jesus I pray. Amen.

EPILOGUE

HOW DOES ANYONE STAYED MARRIED FIFTY YEARS

During the closing months of WW II, the man who was to become my father began exchanging letters with a beautiful, but timid, eighteen-year-old girl named Irene. They could hardly have been less alike. She was a true innocent, having never traveled more than ten miles from her birthplace in Northeastern Colorado, while he was a Navy man having spent much of the war stationed in Hawaii. As the war was winding down in the fall of 1945 he was transferred to the Naval base in Corpus Christi, Texas, and given a two-week furlough. Making his way to Sterling, Colorado, he determined to find out if that dark-eyed beauty was as pretty as her picture.

Not surprisingly it was "love at first sight" and after a whirlwind courtship they were married on November 7, 1945. For sixty-one years, three months and one day they remained completely devoted to one another—a devotion that seems all the more amazing given the social climate in which we now live with its throw-away marriages. When it became impossible for my father to leave his bed during the last week of his life mother remained by his side, taking what little food she ate sitting up in bed beside him. Hour after hour she lay beside him, propping herself up on one elbow so she could look at Daddy. Although we urged her to take a break she refused, saying over and over again, "I promised Daddy I would never leave him and I'm going to stay right here." And that's where she was when Daddy took his last breath and went to be with the Lord.

Had Daddy lived, today would have been their sixty-second wedding anniversary and I can't help but marvel at the love they shared. Following their fiftieth anniversary reception the entire family returned to their home where we shared memories and family stories late into the evening. Finally, my nine-year-old niece snuggled up on the couch beside her grandmother and when there was a pause in the conversation, she asked, "Grandma, how does anyone stayed married for fifty years?"

Her question was raw with the pain caused by her parent's recent divorce and an uneasy silence settled over the room. Pulling her close my mother said, "Honey, Grandpa and I were able to stay married all these years because we could always talk about everything."

That's the key isn't it? Communication—the ability to talk about everything. Not just the easy things but everything—your secret dreams, your hurts, your hopes, your disappointments and even your fears. By talking things through instead of blaming each other and retreating into silence they kept the channels of communication open and strengthened each other and their marriage.

Don't think theirs was an easy marriage for it wasn't, but it was a good one. During their sixty-one years they had some tough things to talk about, the kind of things that would have done a lesser marriage in. Things like financial pressure. Shortly after the folks married Dad went into the water well drilling business but he could never make a go of it. He was under capitalized and his ancient equipment was badly worn and kept breaking down. The thing that finally did him in was a job-related injury that laid him up for weeks. Without insurance or worker's compensation it put him out of business. Refusing to declare bankruptcy, Dad and Mom spent the next several years digging out of debt.

Just weeks before their tenth anniversary Dad and Mom suffered their most devastating blow. Their fourth child, our long awaited baby sister, was born severely hydrocephalic. At birth Carolyn's head was larger than the rest of her body. She wasn't expected to live and even if she did the doctors said she would never be normal.

It seemed each day brought some new disappointment. Soon we realized that Carolyn was both blind and deaf and her head continued to grow more and more disproportionate. With a pain that lingers still, I remember watching Mother as she bathed Carolyn tenderly, then carefully measured her head to see if, by some miracle, it was any smaller. It never was. Mama would bite her lip then, while silent tears ran down her cheeks as she carefully put away the cloth tape measure.

Carolyn died in her sleep, at home, early one morning. Our family doctor and Aunt Elsie arrived at about the same time. He, to make the official diagnosis, and

Aunt Elsie to cook breakfast, which no one ate, and to see after us boys. A short time later, the mortician came and took Carolyn's tiny body away, and the gray December day passed in a maze of necessary activities.

When a child dies it often sounds the death knell for the marriage. Not so for my parents. Although their grief was unspeakable it did not drive them apart. Instead they clung to each other, finding strength in their love. I was reminded of this in the weeks following my father's death. As you might imagine Mother grieved terribly. Once she told me that she didn't think she could make it. In an attempt to encourage her I asked, "How did you make it after Carolyn died?" Without a moment's hesitation she replied, "I had your father to help me. He listened when I needed to talk and when my grief was too deep for words he held me."

Eighteen months after Carolyn's death God blessed Mom and Dad with another child, a beautiful little girl, healthy in every way. But their troubles were not over and in the summer of 1959 Dad severely injured his back while working for Baker Oil Tools, Inc. When it became apparent that the damage was permanent the company gave Dad the choice of transferring to the home office in Houston, Texas, or being terminated. That may seem like a no-brainer but complicating things was the fact that Mother was an only child and the sole caregiver for her elderly mother who was crippled with arthritis. How could she move a thousand miles away and leave her?

Dad suggested that Grandma sell her place and come to Texas with us. A suggestion Grandma quickly vetoed saying, "Dick, there's no house big enough for two women."

To mother she said, "Your place is with your husband. Go to Texas with him. God will take care of me."

So Mom and Dad headed for Houston on a Sunday afternoon in December 1959. That tearful parting is forever etched in my memory. I see Grandma standing by the gate, leaning on her two crutches as she watches us drive away. Dad's back injury is so painful that we have made a bed for him in the backseat of the Buick so he can lie down. Mother is driving and depending on me to help with the younger children. I am only twelve years old but I am the oldest so I must carry my share of the load. I can only imagine the things Mom and Dad talked about late into the night as they prepared to make the biggest move of their lives not knowing what the future might hold.

There's more. In the years ahead Mom and Dad would suffer as two of their children endured the trauma of divorce and all that entails. Dad would undergo two open heart surgeries and suffer from fibrosis of the lungs. Mother's hearing loss, first experienced when she was barely thirty years old, would continue to deteriorate until she could barely hear at all. Because of the fibrosis Dad could only speak in a whisper. They had always talked about everything but now Daddy couldn't talk above a whisper and Momma couldn't hear so they gave up talking for touching. Anytime Momma was within reach Daddy reached out to touch her and she was always caring for him. Truly theirs was a marriage for the ages and an inspiration for those of us who are following in their steps.

When I come to the end of my life I want to have a marriage like that, I want to be more in love with Brenda than ever before. But it won't just happen. A marriage like that is almost always the culmination of a lifelong series of smaller, daily decisions. And as such, it challenges each of us to examine the choices we make each day and the way we relate to each other.

ENDNOTES

CHAPTER 1

[1] Richard Exley, *Blue-Collar Christianity* (Tulsa: Honor Books, 1989), p. 91.

[2] Dr. Frank and Mary Alice Minirth, Dr. Brian and Dr. Deborah Newman, Dr. Robert and Susan Hemfelt, *Passages of Marriage* (Nashville: Thomas Nelson Publishers, 1991). pp. 18,19.

CHAPTER 2

[1] Walter Wangerin, Jr., *As for Me and My House* (Nashville: Thomas Nelson Publishers, 1987), pp. 30,31.

CHAPTER 3

[1] Frederick Herwaldt, Jr., "The Ideal Relationship and Other Myths About Marriage," *Christianity Today,* April 9,1982, p. 10.

[2] Genesis 24:12,14,15,17-19.

[3] Genesis 24:50.

[4] Charlie W. Shedd, *Letters to Karen* (Nashville: Abingdon Press, 1965), pp. 23,24.

CHAPTER 4

[1] James Dobson, *Dr. Dobson Answers Your Questions* (Wheaton: Tyndale House Publishers, Inc., 1982), p. 138.

CHAPTER 5

[1] Erma Bombeck, *A Marriage Made in Heaven or Too Tired for an Affair* (New York: Harper Collins Publishers, Inc., 1993), pp. 3,4.

[2] These questions are adapted from a list prepared by Nick Stinnett, Barbara Chesser and John DeFrain. eds., *Building Family Strengths: Blueprint for Action* (Lincoln: University of Nebraska Press, 1979), pp. 117,118.

[3] Abraham Schmitt, "Conflict and Ecstacy—Model for Manning Marriage," an original paper.

CHAPTER 6

[1] Aaron Rutledge, *Premarital Counseling* (Cambridge: Schenkman, 1966), p. 25.

[2] Matthew 10:39.

[3] Gary Smalley with John Trent, *Love Is a Decision* (Dallas: Word Publishing, 1989). pp. 37,38.

CHAPTER 7

[1] H. Norman Wright, *Seasons of a Marriage* (Ventura: Regal Books, 1982), pp. 9,10.

[2] Ann Landers, "New Rules for the Marriage Game," *Family Circle,* February 3, 1981.

[3] Ephesians 5:22-25.

[4] Rich Buhler, "Learning the Language of Love," taken from *Love: No Strings Attached* and quoted in *The Making of a Marriage* (Nashville: Thomas Nelson Publishers, 1993), p. 87.

CHAPTER 8

[1] Much of the material in this chapter is from *The Making of a Man* by Richard Exley (Tulsa: Honor Books, 1993), pp. 52-55.

[2] These thoughts are based on material from *Marriage Takes More Than Love* by Jack and Carole Mayhall (Colorado Springs: NavPress, 1978), Chapters 24-28.

[3] Madeleine L'Engle, *Walking on Water,* quoted in *Disciplines for the Inner Life* by Bob Benson and Michael W. Benson (Waco: Word Book Publishers, 1985), p. 309.

[4] James 1:5.

[5] Jack and Carole Mayhall, *Marriage Takes More Than Love* (Colorado Springs: NavPress, 1978), p. 186.

[6] Charlie W. Shedd, *Letters to Philip* (Garden City: Doubleday & Company, Inc., 1968), p. 1.

CHAPTER 9

[1] Philippians 4:13.

[2] Philippians 1:6.

[3] Charles R. Swindoll, *Growing Wise in Family Life* (Portland: Multnomah Press, 1988), p. 52.

CHAPTER 10

[1] Proverbs 31:10-12.

[2] Proverbs 31:26.

[3] Ephesians 5:21.

[4] Ephesians 5:22.

[5] James Dobson, *Dr. Dobson Answers Your Questions* (Wheaton: Tyndale House Publishers, Inc., 1982), p. 416.

[6] Ibid., pp. 416,417.

[7] Linda Dillow, "How Can I Know My Man's Unique Needs?" taken from *How to Really Love Your Man* and quoted in *The Making of a Marriage* (Nashville: Thomas Nelson Publishers, 1993), p. 44.

CHAPTER 11

[1] Robert MacNeil, Wordstruck, quoted in "Points To Ponder," *Reader's Digest,* August 1992, p. 167.

[2] Quoted in an article by Barbara Gamarekian in *The Tulsa Tribune,* November 11, 1991.

[3] M. Scott Peck, M.D., *Meditations from the Road* (New York: Simon & Schuster, a Touchstone Book, 1993), p. 125.

CHAPTER 12

[1] M. Scott Peck, M.D., *Meditations from the Road* (New York: Simon & Schuster, a Touchstone Book, 1993), p. 312.

CHAPTER 13

[1] Paul Tournier, *To Understand Each Other,* translated by John S. Gilmour (Richmond: John Knox Press, 1962), p. 29.

[2] Ibid., p. 51.

CHAPTER 14

[1] Genesis 2:24.

[2] Desmond Morris, *Intimate Behavior* (New York: Random House, 1971), p. 73.

[3] Paul Tournier, *To Understand Each Other,* translated by John S. Gilmour (Richmond: John Knox Press, 1962), pp. 28,29.

CHAPTER 15

[1] H. Norman Wright, *Seasons of a Marriage* (Venture: Regal Books, 1982), p. 21.

[2] Howard J. Clinebell and Charlotte H. Clinebell, *The Intimate Marriage* (New York: Harper & Row Publishers, 1970), pp. 99,100.

CHAPTER 16

[1] Howard J. Clinebell and Charlotte H. Clinebell, *The Intimate Marriage* (New York: Harper & Row Publishers, 1970), pp. 95,96.

[2] Walter Wangerin, Jr., *As for Me and My House* (Nashville: Thomas Nelson Publishers, 1987), p. 75.

[3] Ibid., pp. 78,79.

CHAPTER 17

[1] David Mace, *Love and Anger in Marriage* (Grand Rapids: Zondervan Publishing House, 1982), p. 12.

[2] Howard J. Clinebell and Charlotte H. Clinebell, *The Intimate Marriage* (New York: Harper & Row Publishers, 1970), p. 98.

[3] Ibid.

[4] Proverbs 12:18.

[5] M. Scott Peck, M.D., *Meditations from the Road* (New York: Simon & Schuster, a Touchstone Book, 1993), p. 56.

CHAPTER 18

[1] Genesis 2:24.

[2] Dr. Joyce Brothers, quoted in *The Newlywed Handbook* by Yvonne Garrett (Waco: Word Books Publisher, 1981), p. 41.

[3] Dr. Jessie Potter, quoted in *The Newlywed Handbook* by Yvonne Garrett (Waco: Word Books Publisher, 1981), pp. 41,42.

[4] David and Vera Mace, *How to Have a Happy Marriage,* quoted in *Seasons of a Marriage* by H. Norman Wright (Venture: Regal Books, 1982), p. 17.

CHAPTER 19

[1] Howard J. Clinebell and Charlotte H. Clinebell, *The Intimate Marriage* (Now York: Harper & Row Publishers, 1970), p. 99.

CHAPTER 20

[1] Much of the material in this chapter is from *The Making of a Man* by Richard Exley (Tulsa: Honor Books, 1993), pp. 46-49.

[2] Ephesians 4:26 KJV.

[3] H. Norman Wright, *Communication: Key to Your Marriage* (Venture: Regal Books, 1974), p. 145.

CHAPTER 21

[1] Dorothy T. Samuel, *Fun and Games in Marriage* (Waco: Word Books Publisher, 1973), p. 40.

[2] John 8:32.

[3] Genesis 1:27,28,31.

[4] Genesis 2:25.

[5] Hebrews 13:4 KJV.

[6] Walter Wangerin, Jr., *As for Me and My House* (Nashville: Thomas Nelson Publishers, 1987), pp. 189,190.

[7] Proverbs 5:18,19.

[8] I Corinthians 7:3-5.

[9] Walter Wangerin, Jr., *As for Me and My House* (Nashville: Thomas Nelson Publishers, 1987), p. 175.

CHAPTER 22

[1] James Dobson, *What Wives Wish Their Husbands Knew About Women* (Wheaton: Tyndale Home Publishers, Inc., 1975), p. 117.

CHAPTER 23

[1] James Dobson, *What Wives Wish Their Husbands Knew About Women* (Wheaton: Tyndale House Publishers, Inc., 1975).

[2] H. Norman Wright, *Understanding the Man in Your Life* (Waco: Word Books Publisher, 1987).

[3] Michael McGill, *The McGill Report on Male Intimacy* (New York: Harper & Row Publishers, 1985), pp. 188,189.

[4] James Dobson, *What Wives Wish Their Husbands Knew About Women* (Wheaton: Tyndale House Publishers, Inc., 1975), p. 127.

Chapter 24

[1] Charlie W. Shedd, *Letters to Karen* (Nashville: Abingdon Press, 1965).

[2] Charlie W. Shedd, *Letters to Philip* (Garden City: Doubleday & Company, Inc., 1968).

[3] Rich Buhler, "Learning the Language of Love," taken from *Love: No Strings Attached* and quoted in *The Making of a Marriage* (Nashville: Thomas Nelson Publishers, 1993), p. 82.

Chapter 25

[1] Ann Landers, "New Rules for the Marriage Game," *Family Circle,* February 3, 1981.

[2] Howard J. Clinebell and Charlotte H. Clinebell, *The Intimate Marriage* (New York: Harper & Row Publishers, 1970), pp. 140,141.

[3] Ibid., p. 141.

[4] Genesis 2:24.

[5] Genesis 2:20.

[6] Genesis 2:22,25.

[7] Lois Wyse, *Love Poems for the Very Married* (Cleveland: World Publishing Co., 1967), p. 45.

CHAPTER 26

[1] Dave and Claudia Arp, "Learning to Say the 'S' Word or Building a Creative Love Life," taken from *The Marriage Track* and quoted in *The Making of a Marriage* (Nashville: Thomas Nelson Publishers, 1993), p. 178.

[2] James Dobson, *Dr. Dobson Answers Your Questions* (Wheaton: Tyndale House Publishers, Inc., 1982), p. 335.

[3] Walter Wangerin, Jr., *As for Me and My House* (Nashville: Thomas Nelson Publishers, 1987), pp. 112,113.

CHAPTER 27

[1] Richard Exley, *The Rhythm of Life* (Tulsa: Honor Books, 1987).

[2] Walter Wangerin, Jr., *As for Me and My House* (Nashville: Thomas Nelson Publishers, 1987), pp. 248,249.

CHAPTER 28

[1] Dale Carnegie, quoted in *Dawnings: Finding God's Light in the Darkness,* edited by Phyllis Hobe (Waco: Word Books Publisher, 1981), p. 196.

[2] Proverbs 5:18,19.

[3] Aletha Jane Lindstrom, "A Legacy of Rainbows," *Reader's Digest,* December 1984, p. 122.

[4] Walter Wangerin, Jr., *As for Me and My House* (Nashville: Thomas Nelson Publishers, 1987), pp. 248,249.

CHAPTER 29

[1] James Dobson, *Love Must Be Tough* (Waco: Word Books Publisher, 1983), pp. 195,196.

[2] Phyllis Valkins, "A Kiss for Kate," *Reader's Digest,* August 1982, condensed from The Denver Post.

[3] Ibid.

[4] Walter Wangerin, Jr., *As for Me and My House* (Nashville: Thomas Nelson Publishers, 1997), p. 135.

CHAPTER 30

[1] Howard J. Clinebell and Charlotte H. Clinebell, *The Intimate Marriage* (New York. Harper & Row Publishers, 1970), p. 100.

[2] Walter Wangerin, Jr., *As for Me and My House* (Nashville: Thomas Nelson Publishers, 1987), pp. 110,111.

CHAPTER 31

[1] H. Norman Wright, *Seasons of a Marriage* (Ventura: Regal Books, 1982), p. 5.

[2] Ibid., p. 40.

[3] Ibid, pp. 40,41.

[4] Ibid., p. 43.

CHAPTER 32

[1] Some of the material in this chapter was taken from *Perils of Power* (Tulsa: Honor Books, 1988) and other works by Richard Exley.

[2] Lois Wyse, *Are You Sure You Love Me?* (New York: World Publishing, 1969), p. 19.

[3] H. Norman Wright, *Seasons of a Marriage* (Ventura: Regal Books, 1982), p. 104.

[4] Carlfred Broderick, *Couples* (New York: Simon & Schuster, Inc., 1979), p. 161.

[5] Richard Dobbins, "Saints in Crisis," *Grow* (Akron: Emerge Ministries, Inc.), Vol. 13, Issue 1, p. 6.

[6] Ibid., pp. 4,6.

[7] Proverbs 6:27-29,32,33.

[8] R. Kent Hughes, *Disciplines of a Godly Man* (Wheaton: Crossway Books, 1991), p. 32.

CHAPTER 33

[1] H. Norman Wright, *Seasons of a Marriage* (Ventura: Regal Books, 1982), p. 88.

CHAPTER 34

[1] Some of the material in this chapter was taken from *The Making of a Man* (Tulsa: Honor Books, 1993) and other works by Richard Exley.

[2] Jim Conway, *Men in Midlife Crisis* (Elgin: David C. Cook, 1978), p. 17.

[3] H. Norman Wright, *Seasons of a Marriage* (Ventura: Regal Books, 1982), p. 57.

[4] M. Brown, "Keeping Marriage Alive Through the Middle Age," *McCall's,* January 1973, p. 73.

CHAPTER 35

[1] Some material in this chapter was taken from *When You Lose Someone You Love* (Tulsa: Honor Books, 1991) and other works by Richard Exley.

[2] Joe Bayly, quoted in *Training Christians to Counsel* by H. Norman Wright (Denver: Christian Marriage Enrichment, 1977), p. 133.

[3] C.S. Lewis, quoted in *A Severe Mercy* by Sheldon Vanauken (New York: Harper & Row Publishers, 1977), p. 183.

[4] Joshua Liebman, *Peace of Mind* (New York: Simon & Schuster, 1946), p. 109.

[5] Richard Exley, *When You Lose Someone You Love* (Tulsa: Honor Books, 1991), p. 104.

CHAPTER 36

[1] H. Norman Wright, *Making Peace with Your Partner* (Dallas: Word Books Publisher, 1988), pp. 193,194.

[2] H. Norman Wright, *Seasons of a Marriage* (Ventura: Regal Books, 1982), p. 129.

[3] Jim Talley, *Reconcilable Differences,* quoted in *The Making of a Marriage* (Nashville: Thomas Nelson Publishers, 1993), p. 338.

CHAPTER 37

[1] Walter Wangerin, Jr., *As for Me and My House* (Nashville: Thomas Nelson Publishers, 1987), pp. 88,89.

CHAPTER 38

[1] David Augsburger, *Caring Enough to Forgive* (Ventura: Regal Books, 1981), pp. 50,57.

CHAPTER 39

[1] Dr. Richard D. Dobbins, "Saints in Crisis," *Grow* (Akron: Emerge Ministries, Inc.), Vol. 13, Issue 1, p. 8.

[2] Henry A. Virkler, Ph.D., *Broken Promises* (Dallas: Word Books Publisher, 1992), p. 240.

CHAPTER 40

[1] Dr. David Stoop and Jan Stoop, "Nine Myths About Intimacy," taken from *The Intimacy Factor* and quoted in *The Making of a Marriage* (Nashville: Thomas Nelson Publishers, 1993), p. 69.

CHAPTER 41

[1] A poetic form of this piece was included in Richard Exley's *Life's Bottom Line* (Tulsa: Honor Books. 1990), pp. 166,167.

[2] Some of the material in Chapters 41-45 on the Ten Commandments for a Healthy Marriage was taken from *The Rhythm of Life* (Tulsa: Honor Books, 1987), *Perils of Power* (Tulsa: Honor Books, 1988), *Life's Bottom Line* (Tulsa: Honor Books, 1990) and other works by Richard Exley.

[3] Dave and Claudia Arp, "Learning to Say the 'S' Word or Building a Creative Love Life" taken from *The Marriage Track* and quoted in *The Making of a Marriage* (Nashville: Thomas Nelson Publishers, 1993), p. 175.

CHAPTER 42

[1] James Dobson, *What Wives Wish Their Husbands Knew About Women* (Wheaton: Tyndale House Publishers, Inc., 1975), p. 68.

CHAPTER 43

[1] K. C. Cole, "Playing Together: From Couples That Play," *Psychology Today,* February 1982.

[2] Ibid.

[3] G. Robert James, *Michael* (an unpublished work), pp. 288,289.

[4] Charles R. Swindoll, *Growing Strong in the Seasons of Life* (Portland: Multnomah Press, 1983), p. 100.

CHAPTER 44

[1] Ephesians 4:26.27.

[2] James Dobson, *Love for a Lifetime* (Portland: Multnomah Press, 1987), p. 107.

CHAPTER 45

[1] Richard Exley, *Blue-Collar Christianity* (Tulsa: Honor Books. 1989), p. 91.

CHAPTER 46

[1] James Dobson, *Love for a Lifetime* (Portland: Multnomah Press, 1987), pp. 15,16.

[2] Some of the material in this chapter was taken from *Life's Bottom Line* (Tulsa: Honor Books. 1990) and other works by Richard Exley.

[3] Peggy Stanton, *The Daniel Dilemma* (Waco: Word Books Publisher, 1978), pp. 41,43,57.

[4] Genesis 2:18.

[5] Howard J. Clinebell and Charlotte H. Clinebell, *The Intimate Marriage* (New York: Harper & Row Publishers, 1970), p. 18.

CHAPTER 47

[1] Pat Conroy, *The Prince of Tides* (Boston: Houghton Mifflin Company, 1986), p. 23.

[2] Richard Exley, *Life's Bottom Line* (Tulsa: Honor Books, 1990), p. 122.

CHAPTER 48

[1] Some of the material in this chapter was taken from *The Making of a Man* (Tulsa: Honor Books, 1993) and other works by Richard Exley.

[2] R. Kent Hughes, *Disciplines of a Godly Man* (Wheaton: Crossway Books, 1991), pp. 35,36.

[3] Arthur Gordon, *A Touch of Wonder* (Old Tappan: Fleming H. Revell Company, 1974), p. 20.

CHAPTER 49

[1] Some of the material in this chapter was taken from *The Making of a Man* (Tulsa: Honor Books, 1993) and other works by Richard Exley.

[2] John Steinbeck, *Of Mice and Men* (Now York: A Bantam Book published by arrangement with The Viking Press, Inc., 1971), pp. 79,80.

[3] Genesis 2:25.

[4] C. S. Lewis, quoted by Paul D. Robbins in "Must Men Be Friendless?" *Leadership,* Fall Quarter, 1984, p. 28.

[5] I Samuel 18:4.

[6] Walter Wangerin, Jr., *As for Me and My House* (Nashville: Thomas Nelson Publishers, 1987), p. 58.

[7] John M. Hull, *Touching the Rock: An Experience of Blindness,* quoted in "Points to Ponder," *Reader's Digest,* August 1992, p. 168.

CHAPTER 50

[1] Walter Wangerin, Jr., *As for Me and My House* (Nashville: Thomas Nelson Publishers, 1987), pp. 90,91.

BIBLIOGRAPHY

Augsburger, David. *Caring Enough to Forgive.* Ventura: Regal Books, 1981.

Benson, Bob, and Benson, Michael W. *Disciplines for the Inner Life.* Waco: Word Books Publishers, 1985.

Bombeck, Erma. *A Marriage Made in Heaven or Too Tired for an Affair.* New York: Harper Collins Publishers, Inc., 1993.

Broderick, Carlfred. *Couples.* New York: Simon & Schuster, Inc., 1979.

Brown, M. "Keeping Marriage Alive Through the Middle Age," *McCall's,* January 1973.

Clinebell, Howard J., and Clinebell, Charlotte H. *The Intimate Marriage.* New York: Harper & Row Publishers, 1970.

Cole, K. C. "Playing Together: From Couples That Play," *Psychology Today,* February 1982.

Conroy, Pat. *The Prince of Tides.* Boston: Houghton Mifflin Company, 1986.

Conway, Jim. *Men in Midlife Crisis.* Elgin: David C. Cook, 1978.

Dobbins, Robert. "Saints in Crisis," *Grow.* Akron: Emerge Ministries, Inc., Volume 13, Issue 1, 1984.

Dobson, James. *Dr Dobson Answers Your Questions.* Wheaton: Tyndale House Publishers, Inc., 1982.

Dobson, James. *Love for a Lifetime.* Portland: Multnomah Press, 1987.

Dobson, James. *Love Must Be Tough.* Waco: Word Books Publisher, 1983.

Dobson, James. *What Wives Wish Their Husbands Knew About Women.* Wheaton: Tyndale House Publishers, Inc., 1975.

Exley, Richard. *Blue-Collar Christianity.* Tulsa: Honor Books, 1989.

Exley, Richard. *Building Relationships That Last: Life's Bottom Line.* Tulsa: Honor Books, 1990.

Exley, Richard. *Perils of Power.* Tulsa: Honor Books, 1988.

Exley, Richard. *The Making of a Man.* Tulsa: Honor Books, 1993.

Exley, Richard. *The Rhythm of Life.* Tulsa: Honor Books, 1987.

Exley, Richard. *When You Lose Someone You Love.* Tulsa: Honor Books, 1991.

Garrett, Yvonne. *The Newlywed Handbook.* Waco: Word Books Publisher, 1981.

Gordon, Arthur. *A Touch of Wonder.* Old Tappan: Fleming H. Revell Company, 1974.

Herwaldt, Frederick, Jr., "The Ideal Relationship and Other Myths About Marriage," *Christianity Today,* April 9,1982.

Hobe, Phyllis, ed. *Dawnings: Finding God's Light in the Darkness.* Waco: Word Books Publisher, 1981.

Hughes, R. Kent. *Disciplines of a Godly Man.* Wheaton: Crossway Books, 1991.

Hull, John H. "Points to Ponder," *Reader's Digest,* August 1992.

James, Robert. *Michael.* An unpublished work.

Landers, Ann. "New Rules for the Marriage Game," *Family Circle,* February 3, 1981.

Liebman, Joshua. *Peace of Mind.* New York: Simon & Schuster, 1946.

Lindstrom, Aletha Jane. "A Legacy of Rainbows," *Reader's Digest,* December 1984.

Mace, David. *Love and Anger in Marriage.* Grand Rapids: Zondervan Publishing House, 1982.

MacNeil, Robert, "Wordstruck," *Reader's Digest,* August 1992.

Mayhall, Jack, and Mayhall, Carole. *Marriage Takes More Than Love.* Colorado Springs: NavPress, 1978.

McGill, Michael. *The McGill Report on Male Intimacy.* New York: Harper & Row Publishers, 1985.

Minirith, Dr. Frank, and Mary Alice; Newman, Dr. Brian, and Dr. Deborah; Hemfelt, Dr. Robert, and Susan; *Passages of Marriage.* Nashville: Thomas Nelson Publishers, 1991.

Morris, Desmond. *Intimate Behavior.* New York: Random House, 1971.

Peck, M. Scott. M.D. *Meditations from the Road.* New York: Simon & Schuster, a Touchstone Book, 1993.

Robbins, Frank D. "Must Men Be Friendless?" *Leadership,* Fall Quarter, 1984.

Rutledge, Aaron. *Premarital Counseling.* Cambridge: Schenkman, 1966.

Samuel, Dorothy T. *Fun and Games in Marriage.* Waco: Word Books Publisher, 1973.

Schmitt, Abraham. "Conflict and Ecstacy—Model for Maturing Marriage." An original paper.

Shedd, Charlie W. *Letters to Karen.* Nashville: Abingdon Press, 1965.

Shedd, Charlie W. *Letters to Philip.* Garden City: Doubleday & Company, Inc., 1968.

Smalley, Gary with Trent, John. *Love Is a Decision.* Dallas: Word Books Publisher, 1989.

Stanton, Peggy. *The Daniel Dilemma.* Waco: Word Books Publisher, 1978.

Steinbeck, John. *Of Mice and Men.* New York: A Bantam Book published by arrangement with The Viking Press, Inc., 1971.

Stinnett, Nick; Chesser, Barbara; and DeFrain, John; eds., *Building Family Strengths: Blueprint for Action.* Lincoln: University of Nebraska Press, 1979.

Swindoll, Charles R. *Growing Strong in the Seasons of Life.* Portland: Multnomah Press, 1983.

Swindoll, Charles R. *Growing Wise in Family Life.* Portland: Multnomah Press, 1988.

The Making of a Marriage. Nashville: Thomas Nelson Publishers, 1993.

Tournier, Paul. *To Understand Each Other,* translated by John S. Gilmour. Richmond: John Knox Press, 1962.

The Tulsa Tribune, November 11, 1991.

Valkins, Phyllis. "A Kiss for Kate," *Reader's Digest,* August 1982.

Vanauken, Sheldon. *A Severe Mercy.* New York: Harper & Row Publishers, 1977.

Virkler, Henry A., Ph.D., *Broken Promises.* Dallas: Word Books Publisher, 1992.

Wangerin, Walter, Jr., *As for Me and My House.* Nashville: Thomas Nelson Publishers, 1987.

Wright, H. Norman. *Communication: Key to Your Marriage.* Ventura: Regal Books, 1974.

Wright, H. Norman. *Making Peace with Your Partner.* Dallas: Word Books Publisher, 1988.

Wright, H. Norman. *Seasons of a Marriage.* Ventura: Regal Books, 1982.

Wright, H. Norman. *Training Christians to Counsel.* Denver: Christian Marriage Enrichment, 1977.

Wright, H. Norman. *Understanding the Man in Your Life.* Waco: Word Books Publisher, 1987.

Wyse, Lois. *Are You Sure You Love Me?* New York: World Publishing Company, 1969.

Wyse, Lois. *Love Poems for the Very Married.* Cleveland: World Publishing Company, 1967.

AN OPPORTUNITY TO ACCEPT CHRIST

If you have never received Jesus Christ as your personal Lord and Savior, why not do it right now? Simply repeat this prayer with sincerity: "Lord Jesus, I believe that You are the Son of God. I believe that You became man and died on the cross for my sins. I believe that God raised You from the dead and made You the Savior of the world. I confess that I am a sinner and I ask You to forgive me, and to cleanse me of all my sins. I accept Your forgiveness, and I receive You as my Lord and Savior. In Jesus' name, I pray. Amen."

> "...if you confess with your mouth, 'Jesus is Lord,' and believe in your heart that God raised him from the dead, you will be saved. For it is with your heart that you believe and are justified, and it is with your mouth that you confess and are saved.... for, 'Everyone who calls on the name of the Lord will be saved.'"
>
> —ROMANS 10:9,10,13 NIV

> "If we confess our sins, he is faithful and just and will forgive us our sins and purify us from all unrighteousness."
>
> —I JOHN 1:9 NIV

Now that you have accepted Jesus as your Savior:

1. Read your Bible *daily*—it is your spiritual food that will make you a strong Christian.
2. Pray and talk to God daily—He desires for the two of you to communicate and share your lives with each other.
3. Share your faith with others. Be bold to let others know that Jesus loves them.
4. Regularly attend a local church where Jesus is preached, where you can serve Him and where you can fellowship with other believers.
5. Let His love in your heart touch the lives of others by your good works done in His name.

Please let us know of the decision you made. Write:

Vallew Books
P.O. Box 35327
Tulsa, OK 74153-0327

ABOUT THE AUTHOR

Richard Exley, is the author of thirty books, many of them best-sellers, most recently *Man of Valor* and *The Alabaster Cross. The Making of a Man* was a finalist for the prestigious Gold Medallion Award.

His rich and diversified background has included serving as senior pastor of churches in Colorado and Oklahoma, as well as hosting several popular radio programs, including the nationally syndicated *Straight from the Heart.*

When not traveling the country as a speaker, Richard and his wife, Brenda Starr, spend their time in a secluded cabin overlooking picturesque Beaver Lake in Northwest Arkansas.

Richard enjoys quiet talks with old friends, kerosene lamps, good books, a warm fire when it is cold, and a good cup of coffee any time. He's an avid Denver Broncos fan, an aspiring bass fisherman, and an amateur photographer.

To write the author or to schedule speaking engagements, seminars, as well as, men's and couple's retreats, you can contact the author by visiting his website at: www.richardexleyministries.org

You are also invited to listen to the author's daily *Straight From the Heart* podcast, also available on his website.

Additional copies of this book and
other titles by Richard Exley can be ordered
from your local bookstore.

The Alabaster Cross

Man of Valor

Encounters with Christ

Encounters at the Cross (coming soon!)

If this book has touched your life,
we would love to hear from you.

Please write us at:

Vallew Press
P.O. Box 35327
Tulsa, Oklahoma 74153-0327

VALLEW
PRESS